The Lost Supreme

The Lost Supreme

The Life of Dreamgirl Florence Ballard

PETER BENJAMINSON

Lawrence Hill Books

The Library of Congress has cataloged the hardcover edition as follows:
Benjaminson, Peter, 1945-
    The Lost Supreme : the life of Dreamgirl Florence Ballard / Peter Benjaminson. —
1st ed.
    p. cm.
    Includes bibliographical references (p. 201), discography (p. 181), and index.
    ISBN-13: 978-1-55652-705-0
    ISBN-10: 1-55652-705-5
    1. Ballard, Florence, 1943-1976. 2. Singers—United States—Biography.
3. Supremes (Musical group) I. Title.
    ML420.B1336B46 2008
    782.421644092—dc22
    [B]

                                                                2007032949

www.thelostsupreme.com

Interior design: Scott Rattray

© 2009 by Peter Benjaminson
All rights reserved
First edition
Published by Lawrence Hill Books
An imprint of Chicago Review Press, Incorporated
814 North Franklin Street
Chicago, Illinois 60610
ISBN 978-1-55652-959-7
Printed in the United States of America

OTHER BOOKS BY PETER BENJAMINSON

Investigative Reporting
The Story of Motown
Death in the Afternoon
Publish Without Perishing
Secret Police

To Florence Glenda Ballard

1943–1976

And Florence Galinson Benjaminson

1922–2000

AT THE END IS FLORENCE BALLARD. SHE'S THE QUIET ONE.

—*Diana Ross*

THAT'S WHAT *YOU* THINK.

—*Florence Ballard*

Contents

THIS BOOK IS based largely on the author's exclusive audio-taped interview with Florence Ballard, which was conducted over several weeks in 1975. Unless otherwise noted, all quotes from Florence Ballard are from that interview. While every attempt was made to verify the accuracy of Flo's statements, it should be noted that many of them express her personal opinions and feelings, which are by nature subjective and unverifiable.

Preface

Flo and Me

I WAS LOUNGING in the City Room of the *Detroit Free Press* one cold morning in early 1975 when Assistant City Editor John Oppedahl approached me. He was wearing a half-smile that indicated he had recently heard something newsworthy. "I was just told that Florence Ballard is on welfare," he said. "Wanna check it out?" I leaped to my feet. "What!?" I shouted. "A Supreme on welfare!?" At twenty-nine, I was extremely excitable. "Gimme a car and I'll stake out her house until I find her," I said, pounding my desk for emphasis. Oppedahl's half-smile became a grin. He was pleased when his reporters got into their stories.

I drove a *Free Press* staff car, a monstrously powerful Chevy Impala, to the small two-bedroom duplex in Northwest Detroit where John had told me Flo was living. I parked in front of the house, strode purposefully up to the door, and knocked on it. No one was home. I went back to the car and waited. Within forty minutes, Flo and her daughters came walking up the sidewalk. Flo, sporting a neatly trimmed Afro, was wearing a hooded woolen overcoat over a white sweater and a dark pantsuit. She was carrying a bag of groceries. The girls were wearing colorful dresses under their coats and were obviously clean and well cared for. Flo was somewhat startled to see a large, determined-looking man in a suit and topcoat get out of the idling car and approach her, but after I identified myself, she invited me inside.

Although Flo outlined her predicament on that first visit, she didn't seem particularly interested in talking. After I wrote an article about her situation that appeared first in the *Free Press* and then nation- and worldwide, a friend called her and asked, "Why did you tell people you were on welfare? That's a shame." Her reply: "I couldn't very well deny it, because it's the truth, and he knew it."

Flo was pleasantly astounded, however, by the media frenzy and the number of friendly calls the story inspired. So she invited me back to her house to record her life story in her own words. I visited her after work and on weekends over several weeks in 1975 and recorded more than eight hours of tape.

At the time of my visits, when her career was long over, Flo was more statuesque than heavy, with clear skin and a ready laugh. She always dressed casually but neatly. On each occasion, she served me glass after glass of Kool-Aid and talked in a low, pleasant, but somewhat depressed drawl about the ups and downs of her life. The sound of ice cubes tinkling in the Kool-Aid can be heard on the tapes, as well as the sound of her daughters occasionally running through the room, giggling and chasing each other.

I was thrilled to be in contact with such a major celebrity; a poster of the Supremes, including Flo, had decorated my college dorm room for years. We laughed and joked occasionally as she told the happy parts of her story. She recounted the sad parts unhappily, obviously reliving some difficult emotions. It became clear after her death one year later, as those who had been close to Flo began to tell their own stories, that she had left out the very worst parts, either because they embarrassed her or because pain had caused her to suppress some of her memories.

Soon after Flo's death I tried to interest various publications and publishers in her life story; however, public awareness of and interest in her career had declined rapidly after she left the Supremes. Her death revived that awareness briefly, but the decline resumed immediately after her funeral. The success of the Broadway musical *Dreamgirls*, which opened in 1981, caught me napping but inspired Mary Wilson of the Supremes to write her book *Dream-*

girl: My Life as a Supreme. I thought Mary's book had satisfied the newly awak-
ened public interest in both her career and Flo's. But then the opening of the
Dreamgirls movie, twenty-five years later, released a fresh whirlwind of fasci-
nation in the life and career of the Lost Supreme, whose full story had not
yet been told.

Although some of the early portions of my interviews with Flo have been
paraphrased and, to a very limited extent, quoted in some publications, most
of their content has not been revealed until now. Nor has the newest information on Flo, which I obtained through original research, based on clues in
the interviews. I hope you enjoy this joint effort by Flo and me to tell her
side of the story.

Acknowledgments

THANKS TO Randall Wilson, author of the excellent *Forever Faithful!: A Study of Florence Ballard and the Supremes*, who cooperated in the writing of *The Lost Supreme*. A tip of the hat to Flo's sister Maxine Ballard, who published *The True Story of Florence Ballard* in 2007. Kudos and thanks to Mary Wilson, whose 1986 book *Dreamgirl: My Life as a Supreme* began the telling of the Florence Ballard saga.

Thanks to one of my outstanding early editors and one of my oldest friends, John Oppedahl, who assigned the Ballard story to me in 1975 and who has been supporting my pursuit of this and other great stories ever since; to Alan Abrams, who has been supporting my Ballard and Motown efforts since 1977; and to entertainment attorney Jim Lopes, who put it all together.

Additional thanks to the late professor James W. Carey of Columbia University School of Journalism; to the staffs of the Inn on Ferry Street and the Detroit Public Library; to Ruth Miles, the extraordinarily helpful and long-serving Detroit *Free Press* librarian; to *Free Press* and Detroit *News* staffers Judy Diebolt, Peter Gavrilovich, Bill McGraw, and John Smyntek; to the late Neal Shine, the late Linda Ballard, and to Kurt Luedtke; to Dr. Richard "Duke" Hagerty and Dr. Ronald Schwartz; to ace investigator Ed McGrath; to Claudia Menza; to Brian and Melissa Burdick, and to the Skurow brothers, Andrew and Matt.

Thanks also to my friends at my investigative day job, who have been uniformly supportive: Ailsa, Alin, Beatriz, Betty, Carlos, Charlie, Dawn, Emily, Favio, Gerard, Howard, Julie, Julio, Larry, Leo, Lety, Madalyn, Magali, Maria, Mark, Maxima, Milton, Nancy, Pam, Phil, Pilar, Ronald, Selena, Shaela, Suk,

Vincent, Wei, and Yvonne, as well as my also uniformly supportive friends at my previous job, including Annie, Barry, Boomie, Dan, Ed, Goethy, Ming, Pacey, Roger, Salhuddin, Tom, and Vanessa. If I've left out anybody, I promise I'll mention you in my next book.

A tremendous shout-out to my current editors, Yuval Taylor and Lisa Reardon, two of the most thorough, professional, persistent, and indefatigable editors I have ever encountered. Many thanks also for the diligent efforts of sales and marketing coordinator Mary Kravenas and publicists Michelle Niebur and Jen Wisnowski.

And a massive, eternal shout-out to my informal editor in all areas of life, my wife, Susan Harrigan, and to our greatest-ever joint production, Annie Benjaminson, and her husband, ace researcher Greg Naarden.

—Peter Benjaminson, New York City, 2007

Introduction

Founder and Soul Sister

FLORENCE GLENDA BALLARD was the founding member of the Supremes, the most successful female singing group in history. An international singing star by the age of twenty-one, she performed with the other two original Supremes, Mary Wilson and Diane* Ross, before and during their glory years, 1964–1967. Of the fourteen records they recorded during those years, five in a row and ten altogether rose to #1 on the Pop charts. In 1965 and 1966, five of the nine singles they recorded hit #1.

Only the Beatles, the world's other top group at that time, would exceed the Supremes' record, but to maintain their status, the lads from Liverpool had to duke it out with the young women from Motown month after month. While the Fab Four's "Can't Buy Me Love," "Love Me Do," "A Hard Day's Night," and "Penny Lane" climbed the charts to #1, pop perfections such as "Where Did Our Love Go?," "Baby Love," "Stop! In the Name of Love," and "You Keep Me Hangin' On" were right there alongside them.

The trio of singers Florence Ballard brought together was indisputably the most popular group the famed Motown Records Company ever produced.

---

*The name "Diana" was inscribed on Diane's birth certificate by mistake. Her parents had intended to call her "Diane" and did so throughout their lives, as did everyone who knew her. But Diane considered the name "Diana" more glamorous and adopted that name later in her career.

As late as 2006, a drawing of Ballard, Ross, and Wilson—the original Supremes—graced the cover of the Motown History Museum brochure. A banner commemorating "Stop! In the Name of Love" hung on the Detroit museum itself, a memorial to one of Motown's most popular songs.

The Supremes may have made seamless music together, but its members were not at all alike. In the beginning, at least, Flo was the spunky, funny one. Something of a comedienne onstage, she was, said Marvin Gaye, "a beautiful person—loving and warm. . . . She was down-to-earth, she loved to laugh, and everyone loved her." Ex-boyfriend Roger Pearson called her "a great lady, a very proud person, and a person with a lot of dignity. I never heard her say one unkind word about anyone else." Flo's friend and the widow of Motown producer Hank Cosby, Pat Cosby, said, "Flo always greeted me with a smile, and that smile represented who she was."

Flo Ballard had auburn hair and such light skin that her friends called her "Blondie." Beautiful, tall, and statuesque, she was never during her performing years as heavy as the wonderfully talented women who portrayed her in the Broadway and movie versions of *Dreamgirls*.

Mary Wilson was actually the quiet one. Serious and responsible, Mary was determined to survive, and if possible prosper, in what she correctly perceived to be an environment filled with traps and pitfalls.

Diane Ross was a skilled, hard-working, very slender and attractive woman who was, by nearly all accounts, the most determined of the Supremes. Blessed with talent and drive, she was resolved not just to be successful but to be magnificently successful.

There is little disagreement that Florence Ballard had the strongest and most soulful voice of the three Supremes. She could have competed seriously with fellow Detroiter Aretha Franklin, who sang for Atlantic Records. Flo's voice was deep and powerful but had sadness in it too. "Flo was caught between poverty and opulence," said Pearson. "She was only two years out of the projects and into a whole new reality of opulence when she became a star."

It was perhaps this in-between status that allowed Flo to sing both melancholy and cheerful songs with tremendous passion and believability.

During their peak years, the Supremes were a worldwide phenomenon, and the impact of their presence had to be witnessed to be believed. Flo remembered, for example, the reception of the three women when they performed in December 1966 on the island of Barbados.

"We were singing on this barge, or dock, this thing right on the water," Florence said. "They estimated the crowd to be over 100,000 people. So we were singing, and all the plugs and microphones were down where the audience was. These three sailors, I'll never forget, they'd been drinking, so one started it all; and you know how it is in a crowd: all you've got to do is push, and then it's just pushing and pushing and pushing. So we were up there trying to sing, and I see the sailor shove a Barbadian. The Barbadian shoved him. Then they started coming toward us; they started jumping up on the stage.

"We went to run, but there was no place to run. If you went around to the back, there was nothing but water, nothing but the ocean. And we said, 'God, what are we going to do?' They wanted our gowns, a piece of those gowns or the whole gown. They were going to rip it all off. Luckily these guys had these fishing boats, and Berry called them. We got about two of the fishing boats, and we jumped in just in time. They had motors in them, and I was glad of that. Just after we jumped in the boats, they were onstage; they were after us, they were flying, they wanted souvenirs. They missed us by an inch. If they had gotten a hold of us, we would have been naked. The fishing boats took us straight on across the water to the hotel. . . . Berry was the first one in the boat."

"Berry" was the man who was at first Flo's major booster and later her nemesis, Motown Records president Berry Gordy.

Flo Ballard's story has a hopeful beginning, a bright triumph, and a tragic end. Within her short lifetime, she moved from the fringes of American society to its epicenter. Soon after establishing herself there, however, she was catapulted back to the fringes. Despite traveling around the world in luxury, chatting with royalty and heads of state, and being cheered and pursued by millions, Florence Glenda Ballard died, at the age of thirty-two, barely recovered from years of poverty and despair. The purpose of this book is to explain how that happened.

The Lost Supreme

1

Detroit Is Where It's At

"I REMEMBER SINGING," Florence Ballard said.

"I was five years old. I remember singing in churches, at home, and in front of relatives. I even opened a window in the winter and sang out the window, mostly Christmas songs, because it was winter."

Flo was happy. Born on June 30, 1943, in Detroit, Michigan, she was one among many poor black Detroiters, poor enough to be forced to share a bed with four of her sisters and to resign herself to walking to school with holes in her shoes. "I walked real flat so no one could see the holes," she later told *Look* magazine. Still, many black Detroiters were optimistic in the late 1940s and the 1950s as they waited for new worlds to open to them. World War II had brought many blacks—including Flo's father—north to work on auto assembly lines and at other jobs at wages much higher than those their fathers and mothers had earned at hardscrabble labor in the Deep South. The winning of World War II and the consequent expansion of the peacetime auto industry offered the promise of even greater prosperity, in a city free of the South's segregationist laws and, to some extent, its segregationist ways.

Detroit was even a nice place to live. Its downtown has revived somewhat since it emptied out in the 1980s and now boasts two new stadiums, new hotels and condominiums, and a thriving Greektown entertainment district with a new casino. Detroit's neighborhoods have held their own since the 1970s, but the city is still troubled by crime and poverty. Dutch elm disease, the rise of foreign auto industries, the riots of 1967, and ongoing suburbanization made the years from 1967 into the 1990s Detroit's declining years, but all looked bright and open when Flo was young. With its two million people in 1950, Detroit was a metropolis of tree-lined streets that was voted "America's Most Beautiful City" by the U.S. Chamber of Commerce.

Flo's mother was born Lurlee Wilson in Rosetta, Mississippi. Her father was born Jesse Lambert in Bessemer, Alabama. According to Flo, her paternal grandmother was shot in the back when Jesse was an infant, and he was adopted by a family named Ballard. Leaving his adoptive parents when he was thirteen, he hopped trains and hoboed around for a while. He would jump off the train after a day of riding the rails and go to sleep in the nearest graveyard. "He always used to tell us that the best place and the safest place to sleep was in a graveyard," Flo remembered. "You can imagine what I said! Have I ever slept in a graveyard? Are you joking? No way! I don't even look at them."

"While he was hoboing," Flo said, "he met my mother, when she was about fourteen. They got married, and she started having babies and never stopped." The couple moved to Detroit in 1929 and eventually had thirteen children, of which Flo was the eighth.

Like any other father with so many children, Jesse Ballard was forced to be a stern disciplinarian at times. On one occasion, according to Flo, "I was about an hour late coming home, and Mary [Wilson] and I were supposed to go to a record hop. I rushed into the house and was getting ready to change clothes. My father said, 'No, you can't go—you've been late coming home from school; you have to stay home.' That did it. I went upstairs and tore the sheet off the bed and started tearing up other things. He came up there and whipped my butt, and that ended that forever."

On another occasion, she recalled, "I threw a pipe at my sister. It hit the porch, ricocheted, and knocked the kitchen window out, and he knocked the hell out of me." Apparently he didn't spank her too hard. "I was spoiled," she said. "He spoiled me. I was the baby girl at one time until Linda and Pat were born, and now Linda's the baby girl, but I always felt I was closer to him than anyone. When I was four years old, I used to crawl up in the bed with him. I didn't want to sleep with anyone else; I wanted to sleep with my father." Her major memory involving her father was falling repeatedly out of her own bed and being gently lifted back into it by her loving dad. Flo's sister Maxine wrote in her self-published book, *The True Story of Florence Ballard*, that Jesse Ballard had a problem with alcohol, but Flo never mentioned it.

Jesse Ballard spent most of his life working at General Motors. He had started working there at age twenty or twenty-one. "He'd always have on his black pants and his red-and-white checked shirt or his black-and-white checked shirt. It was either one or the other. He'd go to work and come home to his family and then just sit until the next day," Flo said. But while he sat, he often played the blues on his old, boxlike string guitar. And Flo sat on his knee and listened. Sometimes, she sang.

After thirty years on the line, according to Flo, GM gave her dad a gold watch. "That was great—wow!—a gold watch," Flo said sarcastically.

The Ballard family would live in various places in Detroit, one of them a building that Flo called a "shelter for the poor" on East McDougall* in Black Bottom, then a teeming, mostly black ghetto on the lower east side of Detroit. (These days the neighborhood is host to a successful racially and economically diverse low-rise housing project.) The family stayed there when Flo was eight or nine.

"The only people who stayed in that shelter were people with large families or people who were poor and couldn't afford to do any better," Flo said. "We slept here and there," in the small space they shared on McDougall. "There were five girls in one bed, five sisters, and maybe three brothers in

---

*Most Detroit streets and avenues are referred to by their name only, without the addition of the word "Street" or "Avenue."

another bed." Although Jesse Ballard received a relatively large salary working on the assembly line, with so many kids at home it couldn't be stretched far enough to keep the family out of a shelter.

"My mother once told me, 'If they had had all these things on the market when I was younger, to prevent pregnancy, I wouldn't have had all these children,'" Flo said. "But I think my mother wanted a lot of children."

A large family suited Flo, who enjoyed her brothers and sisters. Her sister Bertie, the Ballards' first child, was twenty years older than Flo. Then came her eldest brother, Cornell, followed by Jesse Jr., Gilbert, Geraldine, Barbara, Maxine, Flo, Billy, Calvin, Pat, Linda, and Roy. But tragedy as well had struck the Ballard family. Before Flo was born, her mother had given birth to twins who had died at the age of five months and a girl who had died in infancy. And Flo's youngest brother, Roy, was killed by a drunk driver at the age of three.

Late at night, Flo and the other kids would run around pretending they were ghosts and scaring one another. "I woke up one night and Billy and Calvin had this sheet over their head, and they were saying they were ghosts," Flo remembered. "I said, 'If you're a ghost, then I can run right through you.' So I went running right into them and trampled them to death. I'll never forget that."

Flo wasn't the only artist in the family. Each of the brothers and sisters was a musician in his or her own way. Family jam sessions were common. Billy would demand the lead almost all of the time. "He couldn't really sing, but he'd be thinking he was really singing. That cracked us up," Florence said. When relatives came over, they'd often give the kids a dime to sing.

From an early age, Flo clearly saw herself as a solo performer as well as a member of a singing group. "My favorite song was 'Silent Night,'" she said. "Seemed like every winter I was pulling up the window and singing that. My voice was real high-pitched, and people used to tell me, 'I heard you singing last night, and you sounded pretty,' and that made me lift the window up even more."

Flo's parents, although not regular churchgoers themselves, pushed their children into organized religion via a storefront Baptist church on Detroit's East Side. A man Flo remembered as Rev. Williams would come by in his old black station wagon every Sunday and, to Flo's amazement, not only drive Flo and her siblings to church but also pay them, in small change or in candy and ice cream, for attending services. Attracted by such fine treatment, Flo was baptized, sang in the choir, attended services, and was singing by herself in front of church audiences by the time she was five years old.

The building where the family lived on East McDougall was four stories high. "I used to slide out the window and sit on the fire escape. It was always hot in there," Flo said. From her perch she could observe one teenage boy after another hopping over the little cement wall after the 10:00 P.M. curfew. "I used to turn handflips against the same wall. . . . I was nice and skinny and carefree," Flo said.

"One day," Flo said, "we were all together playing, and I got lice in my head. I didn't know what lice were. My mother took me in the house, and she said, 'I see something in your hair,' because she used to comb my hair all the time. I said 'What!?' And she said, 'You've got lice in your head.' I said, 'Lice!?' and started trembling and got real nervous. I could see her picking these things out and putting them on paper. Then she filled my head up with some kind of DDT or some stuff. I said, 'Where do they come from?' And she said, 'White people have them in their hair.' The kind of white people we lived around weren't so clean. I had caught lice from the white children I played with. Mother went next door and told the lady about it, so then that lady checked her kids' heads, and she found out that they had lice too."

Soon after Flo's sister Pat's birth, the family moved, first to another housing project on Ethel in southwest Detroit, then to still another project on Eight Mile Road, the northern border of Detroit that Eminem later made famous.

Flo's description of the Eight Mile Road project as "cardboardlike" probably made an incident that occurred there seem more threatening than it was.

An old stove sat in the living room, which Flo's father fed with wood and coal every day. "We didn't have a furnace, just an old stove sitting in the living room that went all the way up to the ceiling. Every day my father would be putting coal and wood in it. . . . I walked past that stove one day, and my sleeve got caught on the stove door—and I jerked, and I burned my whole arm. I'll never forget that stove as long as I live." Nevertheless, she enjoyed her new home, partly because her family, which she considered stupendously large, was surrounded by even larger ones. A family across from her, the Moores, boasted sixteen children, putting Flo's family of thirteen kids into some sort of perspective.

Flo's warm family, and her secure place in it, made her happy, generous, and gregarious. It also made her determined to hold on to whatever she gained in life, partly because she felt loved and valuable and believed she deserved whatever good came her way. But being a middle child in a large family, she also learned early on that she had to speak up to get the attention she firmly believed she deserved and that she had to continue to speak up about her grievances at all costs if she wanted to avoid being overwhelmed by the needs and ambitions of others.

Flo was also particularly protective of her relatives. She aided them in the earliest days of their lives and would continue to aid them financially and otherwise later, when her income began to grow. Flo recalled that when she was still a child, "I was holding my baby sister Linda in my arms. She was about nine months old, and I was about ten. I was sitting on the porch, just rocking her, because I love babies, when a little white boy walked up and threw a rock that just missed her head. So I laid her in her crib, and I took off after him. He got inside his fence and told his father, 'That black girl is after me! And she's trying to beat me up!' His father came out and said, 'You better leave him alone, you little black boy.' He thought I was a boy because I always wore blue jeans then—my mother called me tomboyish—and my hair was pinned up. So I walked back home and told my mother. She said she thought the boy's father should have chastised him for throwing that rock. Then the father came over and started cursing us and carrying on and talking like he was really going to beat my butt. Another white guy, Paul Ayers, who lived next to us, heard him and came over from next door and told him, 'Look, cool it. You don't talk to people like that.' The father started calling Ayers 'you nigger lover' and this and that. He kept on running his mouth, so Paul hit him and knocked him out. He got up after a while and went home, and we had no more problems out of him."

During the 1950s the Ballards moved to the Brewster Projects, a gleaming new public housing project that was a fine place to live at the time. Flo recalled the family's bright and shining two-story row house, complete with four bedrooms, varnished floors, a basement, and a modern kitchen. But she didn't remember the Brewster Projects just because it was the best place she had ever lived. It was there that she met Mary Wilson and Diane Ross, and it was there that her public life began.

Like Flo, young Mary Wilson loved to sing. They both sang in church choirs and once performed at the same school talent show. After congratulating each other, the two girls started walking to school together. They attended the same elementary and junior high schools but would go on to different high schools, Mary to Northeastern and Flo to Northwestern.

"Mary was a skinny, homely little girl. I guess I must have been too," Flo said. In truth, earlier in her life, Flo had indeed been a skinny, homely little girl, but soon after she and Mary became friends, in 1958, Flo began to grow up. She became a tall young woman with long legs and auburn hair. She also had a big bust, large and sensuous lips, and an attractively pointed chin.

Flo, who was very interested in the dress and appearance of everyone she knew—male or female—throughout her life, added that Mary "had only one sister and one brother, so her mother was able to buy more clothes for her, and Mary was always sharp; boy, Mary was always sharp."

Mary was different from Flo in other ways as well. Born in Mississippi, she had been sent north to be raised by her aunt and uncle in Detroit while her parents and their other children stayed down south. The aunt who raised her, Mary said, believed that children should be seen but not heard. When Mary was eleven, her mother moved to Detroit with two younger children, and Mary moved in with her relocated mother, brother, and sister. Living with stern relatives who were not her parents for the first decade of her life, and then having to join an already established family at age eleven, prepared Mary to survive the subsequent massive changes in her life and also taught her to remain quiet and keep many of her thoughts to herself, no matter what the provocation. "I learned to keep my mouth shut," she said. She contrasted strongly with the outspoken Flo.

The singing classes that Flo and Mary took in school educated their voices. (One of the reasons Detroit produced so many singers in the 1950s and '60s was because of the extensive music program its public schools offered.) "You're supposed to sing from your stomach," Flo said, "not from your throat. And in order to breathe from your stomach, you have to breathe in, and as you're singing, you breathe out. Mr. Silvers, my vocal teacher in high school, always used to tell me, 'Drop your jaws.' You drop your jaws all the way down, and I swear I had earaches for weeks and weeks. It felt like knots were under my ears from dropping my jaws. When you drop your jaws, your tongue goes down to the bottom part of your mouth, it folds under, and then you sing."

Flo may have complained about her teacher, but those earaches would soon pay off.

2

Generosity and Betrayal

Yeah, I know a girl that can sing:
Mary, Mary Wilson.

—Florence Ballard, 1959

THE DETROIT OF the late 1950s and early 1960s wanted live entertainment and had the money to pay for it. The city boasted a pool of talented young singers and musicians, including the teenage Flo Ballard. A number of entrepreneurs soon appeared, hoping to unite the singers and the audiences and profit in the process.

Milton Jenkins was one such entrepreneur. Born into a family of thirteen children in Birmingham, Alabama, Jenkins had gone north to make his fortune in the music business and had situated himself in its Michigan epicenter, a residential hotel across the street from Detroit's Flame Show Bar. In many ways, Jenkins was a model entertainment impresario, with the requisite interest in flash and dash. He invested every dollar he could spare to make his groups look good and drove them to their gigs in his own Cadillac. When he met Flo, his major group was a male trio called the Primes. Jenkins was optimistic about them, but girl groups were also becoming popular, so Jenkins figured he'd recruit a sister group. Naturally, they'd be called the Primettes.

Many of Jenkins's contemporaries formed and managed a few groups that faded away after short careers. But something inspired Milton Jenkins. By creating the Primes, which became the Temptations, and the Primettes, which became the Supremes, Jenkins helped create and was the first manager of not just one but two of history's most popular singing groups.

Jenkins began looking around for some young female singers. Flo's sister Maxine told Jenkins that Flo could really sing. Jenkins wanted to hear Flo, so in early 1959 he invited her over to his residential hotel, which was not too far from the Brewster Projects, to sing for him and two of the Primes, Eddie Kendricks and Paul Williams. (All three Primes, including Kell Osborne, lived with Jenkins in his apartment.)

Maxine took Flo over there, and, as Flo said simply, "I stood there and sang one of the songs from the '50s." But there was much more to it than that. Flo knew instinctively that this was an important moment. If Jenkins rejected her and found other girls for his group, or if he abandoned the whole idea of a girl group, her career might be over forever.

Flo rose to the challenge. What Jenkins saw and heard that day was what people in the music business call "the real deal." As a witness to one of Flo's early performances told author J. Randy Taraborrelli, "She gave it her all, hitting the high notes, holding them with perfect pitch, selling the song . . . giving the total entertainer's package." Jenkins was impressed. He immediately asked her if she knew any other young women who could sing. "I said, 'No,'" Flo remembered, "then 'Yeah, I know a girl that can sing: Mary, Mary Wilson.'" Jenkins asked Flo to bring Mary back with her. If Mary sang as well as Flo did, Jenkins said, the two would be the nucleus of a new singing group.

Mary remembers Flo running up to her in a school hallway, out of breath, and telling her about this astounding offer. According to Mary, while Flo panted out the details, she gripped Mary's arm very tightly, so tightly it almost hurt. There was no suspenseful period of consideration. As soon as Mary heard the word "singing," she said yes.

When Flo and Mary returned to Jenkins's apartment, Paul Williams was the only one there. Williams asked them if they knew any songs, Flo began singing "Night Time Is the Right Time," and Mary joined in. Williams liked what he heard, and the Primettes were born.

In the musical hothouse that was Detroit, when Flo and Mary returned to the Brewster Projects, they were greeted by the sounds of numerous other groups singing on street corners. At least in the minds of the youngsters who hoped to be its future participants, Detroit's music world was booming. Maybe it wasn't just wishful thinking. Pat Cosby insisted that in the Detroit of that era "even the smallest clubs featured topflight entertainment."

Flo and Mary soon recruited another member for the group, Betty McGlown (who later married and became Betty Travis), after auditioning several other young women who didn't make the grade. McGlown didn't live in the same neighborhood as Flo and Mary but had heard through the grapevine that they were looking for singers. A few days later, Paul Williams heard the young Diane Ross singing on some porch steps with some friends, told her about the group in formation, and brought her over to meet Flo, Mary, and Betty.

Although Diane lived in the same neighborhood as Flo and Mary, she went to different schools. An interest in fashion design would lead her to Detroit's Cass Technical High School. Her experience with music until that time had not been as successful as had the other girls'. Diane took a singing class at her school, but she dropped out when it became evident she would get a D. While she never had another singing class, she was by all accounts driven to succeed at whatever she did, and as her life came into focus, she decided she would succeed at singing.

Thus Florence Ballard founded the Primettes, later renamed the Supremes. Flo would call the creation of the world's most successful female singing group the major achievement of her life, and in the beginning, she was indeed its undisputed leader. She was older than Mary and Diane and sang with a full, warm, gospel-tinged voice that was stronger than theirs. "It was Flo's voice that put us over," Mary said.

"Every evening after school, we'd be rehearsing," Flo said. "Not making any money—just rehearsing." Soon, Williams taught the quartet "The Twist," on which Flo took the lead, and "There Goes My Baby," which Diane led. He also taught them the first of the onstage routines the Supremes would make legendary over the years.

But before the group began performing in public, Flo's parents had second thoughts. They wanted her to be successful in life, and to them that meant being successful in school. Singing, rehearsing, and performing with her friends would hardly help her get good grades. Diane and Mary visited Flo's house many times to convince her parents that they'd make sure she studied and did her homework if the Ballards would allow her to sing with them. Eventually, they were successful. Ironically, Diane later criticized Flo's parents for selfishly wanting Flo to be a singer more than Flo herself wanted it.

The group began to perform at Detroit clubs and cabarets, church recreation rooms, and union halls, singing such standards as "There Goes My Baby" and "Night Time Is the Right Time." Although Flo's strong, deep voice was the dominant one, the lead passed democratically from one girl to the other, depending on who the group decided would be the best in that role for each song. At most of the small venues they played, the house supplied the food—sandwiches, hot sausages, fried chicken—and the patrons brought their own liquor. The Primettes were too young to sing legally in a club that had a liquor license. Betty McGlown was the old lady of the group, at seventeen; Flo was fifteen; and Diane and Mary were fourteen.

The teens dressed their age. Diane and her mother made balloon dresses for the group—big-skirted orange dresses that would puff out over the body and then be reeled back in by elastic around the legs. Their alternate outfits were stretched-out red or white sweaters bearing the letter "P" for Primettes, white pleated skirts, sweat socks, and white gym shoes, which eventually turned gray from wear.

In Flo's words, the Primettes were "sharp" and "out of sight" of any competitors. "They were throwing money at us." She was telling the literal truth.

"The audience would be drinking," and, according to Flo, "they'd say, 'What the hell, they sound good; let's give 'em all our money!' They'd put money down on the stage at our feet. Don't think we didn't pick it up. The next day, they'd wake up sober and say, 'Where the hell did all our money go?'"

Neither Flo nor the other Primettes can be blamed for picking up all the money thrown at them. Their pay, which Jenkins gave them, was fifteen dollars for the group for each performance, plus tips. What the club owners and church recreation people paid Jenkins is lost in the mists of rock 'n' roll history, but considering the venues the group played, it's unlikely he made much if anything on them. (Jenkins died in 1970.) And he did buy their clothes, or the material with which Diane and her mother made their clothes. Like Motown in later years, he probably felt justified charging such expenses to the group's account.

In any case, the Primettes were hardly in a mood to care about such things. "We weren't thinking about the money then," Flo said. Less than four dollars each was relatively unimportant compared with having people admire them. "It was something new, something to do, rather than sit around the hot projects," Flo said.

In the midst of this exciting time for Flo, tragedy struck. Her beloved father, Jesse Ballard, died in 1959 from cancer, at age fifty-four. It was a major blow to young Flo. "Diane Ross sang at his funeral," Flo recalled, "and she said that was the last funeral she would ever sing at, because it shook her up too much.

"My father was lowered in the ground, and I cried and cried because he was gone forever," Flo said. "A lot of nights I'd wake up and think that he was still there. Ever since then, I don't like to go to funerals. If I do go, I never go to the cemetery, because I don't want to see anybody lowered into the ground."

With the insurance and Social Security money the family received as a result of her husband's death, Flo's mother moved them out of the Brewster Projects in late 1960, into a single-family house on Spokane, near Grand River, in a residential section of Detroit.

Despite her sadness, Flo's obsession with singing never faltered. She continued to sing out the window, with her brothers and sisters, in church, in the glee club, at school concerts, when she was all alone, and with the Primettes. "I would be in the classroom, and my mind would just jump straight out the window. Singing—that was on my mind, and I couldn't shake it," she said.

As Flo became better known in the neighborhood for her singing, she acquired her first boyfriend, an aspiring musician named Jesse Greer. Jesse had founded another singing group, the Peppermints, which was featured at Detroit's Flame Show Bar and the Twenty Grand Lounge. Flo would show her devotion to Jesse by watching his group perform, and Jesse reciprocated by going to watch the Primettes' rehearsals. He immediately noticed two weaknesses in the group: he felt that Diane sang through her nose, and told her not to, and he told Mary to project her voice more.

Jesse also noted that Flo was not only the group's natural leader but also the best singer of the four. He shared with the girls his opinion that if Flo sang more leads, the group would make it to the big time. He taught them some ballads, and the girls spent hours perfecting the intricate harmonies of the tunes he suggested. Eventually, however, Flo and Jesse Greer drifted apart.

After two years of singing locally, the Primettes began to tire of performing for next to nothing and going nowhere. They wanted to make a record, have all their friends hear it, sing it to adoring throngs at packed concerts, and ride around in limos. They wanted fame, and cutting a record was the only way to become big-time singers. As Mary put it, "No records, no career." They kept asking Jenkins to hook them up with a recording company, but he couldn't or wouldn't. All Jenkins seemed to be able to do was get local gigs.

Then, in the summer of 1960, someone who knew someone saw the Primettes singing in a church recreation room and told Motown Records they looked promising. Motown songwriter Richard Morris asked them in to audition.

Motown Record Company would soon alter American music and American attitudes permanently. It was the linchpin in the successful struggle launched by black musicians and black music executives to stop whites from stuffing their pockets with the millions of dollars that resulted from the sales of tunes written, sung, and often produced by blacks.

Motown was founded by Berry Gordy, one of eight children who inherited their highly entrepreneurial parents' interest in business and in getting ahead. As a child and adolescent, Gordy had resisted helping his father in his plastering business, print shop, and grocery store. Nor did he join his mother in her insurance business and political activities. He insisted instead on picking out tunes on the piano in the Gordys' basement and singing in talent shows, and he went his own way competitively by becoming a boxer, probably the most independent move he ever made.

Five feet six inches tall, and thin, Gordy started as a flyweight; he worked and grew his way to bantamweight and finally featherweight (126 pounds). He then dropped out of high school and turned pro, slugging it out all over America for two years until he realized that no matter how well he did, lightweight boxing champs in the United States are neither rich nor famous. Gordy wanted to be both. Besides, one of his pals at the gym was Jackie Wilson, who had musical ambitions.

After spending two uneventful years as an army draftee, Gordy started his musical career by opening a jazz record store in Detroit with his army savings and some borrowed money. He loved jazz but there wasn't enough of a local market for jazz recordings to support his store, and it went bankrupt within a year or two. From then on he vowed to concentrate on what music consumers liked when he was putting musical products on the market.

Noting the growing music scene in Detroit, which had already swept up Flo Ballard and her friends, Gordy started writing songs for Jackie Wilson, who had started to sing commercially. Four of the five songs he wrote—"Reet Petite," "To Be Loved," "I'll Be Satisfied," and "That's Why"—were hits. The fifth song, "Lonely Teardrops" (1958), was not only a hit but a monster hit. It was the story of a million teenage lives. Gordy had established himself as a songwriter, but he hadn't yet achieved fame or fortune.

Gordy soon realized that he was no more going to get rich as a songwriter than as a boxer. On his wall he hung the $3.19 royalty check that was his entire payment for one of his hit records—just to remind him of this fact. While peddling songs to various singers, he had become aware that there were many vocalists in Detroit looking for not only songs to sing but also record contracts to make them rich. He took the hint and became a record producer, selling the master recordings he produced to record companies in New York City.

Still, Gordy's profit margin remained razor thin. His major preoccupation in those days was reflected in one of the hit records he wrote around this time: "Money (That's What I Want)." (Gordy was not subtle, at least not in his songwriting.) Finally, his pal Smokey Robinson allegedly told him, "Why work for the man? Why not *you* be the man?" Gordy borrowed eight hundred dollars from his family's financial co-operative and opened the Motown Record Company. (The source, or sources, of the other capital Gordy must have received has never been disclosed.) The company would both record the master records and manufacture the records themselves.

Gordy moved the relatives who were willing to work for him, plus a handful of other young Detroiters he had recruited with promises and very small salaries, into a collection of seedy brick houses with front porches and shingled walls on both sides of a heavily traveled street in central Detroit. He used these houses as office buildings. The neighborhood had once been wealthy— the street was named West Grand Boulevard—but by 1959 it was a slightly run-down, middle-class area near General Motors headquarters in Detroit. Gordy converted the tiny rooms in the aging houses, including a basement toilet, into Motown's recording studios.

Keenly aware of both his small budget and his talent for producing popular records, Gordy decided that the only way his small company would succeed before it ran out of money was to produce only hits. By "hits," Gordy didn't mean the Top 100; he meant the Top 10—and not on the Rhythm and Blues chart, the back of the bus of the record business, but the Pop, or popular music, chart, where white hits, or black records that became white hits, were listed. This was a startling goal, since some 80 percent of all records produced at the time neither became hits nor even recovered the money that had been spent to produce them. But Gordy was adamant. To emphasize his new policy, he hung a sign on the house that was his corporate headquarters, reading "Hitsville, USA."

Gordy had strong feelings about what went into a hit song. He believed songs needed to tell stories rather than just spout a lot of sounds. He also believed lyrics should be written in the present tense, so that people on the street, rushing to and fro, could easily relate to them: "Not 'My girl broke up with me' but 'My girl's breaking up with me,'" Gordy told a Motown songwriter. He also produced his records so they would sound their best on the tinny car radios of the time, rather than on home stereo systems. Other record companies in Detroit did not concentrate as much on the car radio as Gordy did.

Gordy's hit-making skills were impressive. On several occasions, he changed a few chords around in a song and moved it from loser to hit status. And he was rough on songwriters. He rejected the first one hundred songs his bosom buddy Smokey Robinson wrote. Constrained by both his budget and his perfectionism, he released very few of the songs his producers taped and presented to him. When Florence and her pals were performing in local dives, Gordy was working his way toward what would become Motown's astounding score in its glory days: one in three records the company released at its height was a hit. No other record company even came close to that statistic.

Florence remarked that by 1960 she "had heard a little bit about Motown and Berry Gordy. Someone—it may have been Diane's father—said something wasn't right about him." What Mr. Ross may have heard was that Mary Wells and other artists were already criticizing Gordy for allegedly cheating them out of their royalties. Recalling this "something wasn't right" remark in 1975, Flo added, "I know it's true now, looking back; I know it's true—it's a fact."

Nevertheless, in the summer of 1960, Florence Ballard and her three friends took a bus over to the two-flat on West Grand Boulevard that served as Motown's headquarters, recording studio, and offices and auditioned for Richard Morris, Motown producer Robert Bateman, and Gordy himself. They sang "There Goes My Baby," "Night Time Is the Right Time," "The Twist," and "There's Something on Your Mind." According to various observers, Diane's lead vocal was unimpressive, Flo whispered to Mary about Motown's shady reputation, and Mary stayed silent except when singing.

Gordy's reaction, Flo said, was "We can't give you a recording contract now. Come back after you finish school." He was being diplomatic. Neither law nor custom required Motown to record only high school graduates, and the company would later do quite well with high school students as singing stars: three of the four Marvelettes were still in high school when their "Please Mr. Postman" went to #1 on the charts. Gordy himself hadn't graduated from high school. And when the Primettes eventually began recording for Motown as the Supremes, three of them were still in high school.

Some have said that Gordy put off the Primettes because he already had a hot female group, the Marvelettes, and didn't want his company typecast. Others said he was somewhat wary of having four female minors around. Still others said the Primettes needed more experience and Gordy knew it. All are possible, but the most likely explanation is that Gordy and company didn't like Diane's singing style. Robert Bateman, one of the Motown producers present at the audition, expressed this view most succinctly: "Who wants a girl who sings through her nose?" he asked.

Richard Morris, however, thought the Primettes would be successful in the long run and was willing to take over their management to help them get the experience he thought they needed. He did this as a side job with Motown's permission. The teens had a contract with Jenkins that should have made it impossible for Morris to manage them without Jenkins's written consent, but they disregarded it. Although Florence later blamed it on ignorance, it was one of the only occasions during a very public life when she did something that truly lacked class. "We didn't know anything about contracts," Flo said. "We said, 'Hell, we signed some papers, so?' We wanted to make a record. . . . It was a written contract, but evidently it didn't mean anything. . . . Anyway, Jenkins never bothered us for leaving. He just let us go."

Jenkins still had the Primes, but later, seeing the shape of the future and also wanting to record, they too slipped out of his life and migrated to Motown. But Jenkins couldn't have been *that* upset: after the Primettes became the Supremes, he married Flo's sister Maxine. Maxine told Flo, however, that Jenkins was angry. "I would help him, whenever I could," Flo said of her contacts with Jenkins after the group broke their contract with him, "but that was that."

The Primettes' cavalier attitude about contracts worked to their advantage at this point, but it would certainly work to their disadvantage later when they realized, too late, that Motown took its contracts a lot more seriously.

Morris, whose connections were better than Jenkins's, arranged for the Primettes to do some background singing for vocalists Eddie Floyd and Wilson Pickett, both just starting their solo careers and recording at Detroit's Flick & Contour Studios. At the recording session, some secrets of economical record making were revealed: the Primettes, before being allowed to make their own very first recording on their very first day at the studio, were required to do background singing for other artists' records without pay.

On one side of their own record, finally produced on the LuPine label, was "Tears of Sorrow," on which Diane sang the lead, and on the flip side the ballad "Pretty Baby," on which Mary led, although Flo's voice overpowered the voices of the other three on both sides of the disc. The record, released in 1960, went nowhere. The "Tears of Sorrow" side was played on the radio only once. Flo guessed correctly that neither Morris, West, nor LuPine had the money or experience to push the record into the big time. It was hardly an auspicious beginning.

By 1975, Flo had forgotten "Tears of Sorrow." She had also given away her only copy of that record. "As a matter of fact," she said, "I can't keep a record. I used to have stacks and stacks of albums, Supremes and all. But people would come by and say, 'May I have your album?' and I'd give them the album. They wanted them autographed too. So I ended up without any albums."

Although Morris never put out a hit by the Primettes, he did get the group better gigs than Jenkins did. The Primettes were invariably the opening act; however, they opened at prestigious local venues such as the Graystone Ballroom.

Diane became more and more headstrong as the group gained popularity, but the older Betty McGlown, working with Morris, was able to hold her in check on most occasions. One of the restrictions that angered Diane most was Morris's refusal to allow any of the young women to mingle with the customers. Morris was well aware that they were attractive, naive, and underage—catnip to their male fans—but Diane often defied him. A few years later it would be Diane, ironically, who would sneer at Florence for mingling with people.

In July 1960 Betty announced she was leaving the group to get married. Flo and her remaining two costars were shattered by the news and tried to convince her to stay with them. But it had long been obvious to the others that Betty saw the group as only a pastime, unlike Ballard, Ross, and Wilson, who saw the group as life itself. Although all four remained friendly, Flo, Mary, and Diane were devastated by Betty's defection, partly because they believed that a successful group needed four members.

It was in 1960, while the Primettes were recovering from this disappointment, that Flo endured one of the worst experiences of her life. As Mary Wilson wrote in *Dreamgirl*, she and Diane first realized that something was wrong when Flo, whose ear might as well have been attached to her home telephone receiver, stopped returning their calls and her mother told them that Flo didn't want to sing with them anymore. Mary and Diane couldn't believe that the founder and organizer of the group—someone they knew valued singing above almost all else—had abandoned her singing career. But they were well aware that Flo did value one thing above singing—family—and that Flo's mother had been worried for months about the group's taking time from Flo's schoolwork and blighting her future.

For weeks the group neither rehearsed nor performed. When Flo finally answered one of their daily phone calls and then met with Mary and Diane, after two months of isolation at home, they realized something terrible had occurred. She was exhausted and unkempt and refused eye contact. When she opened her mouth, she began to talk, then began to cry, and then began talking again. She finally blurted out the full story.

According to Mary Wilson, one pleasant summer evening during 1960, Flo had attended a sock hop at the Graystone Ballroom. Flo's mother didn't usually let any of her daughters go out alone, but this event seemed safe enough. No alcohol was served, and Flo's brother Billy was going with her.

During the evening, however, Flo became separated from Billy. As the sock hop wound down, she stood near the door of the ballroom, hoping to find Billy and go home with him. When she heard someone call her name from a car outside, she thought it was her brother and ran to the car. It wasn't Billy in the car, but she recognized the young man as someone she knew. She got in.

Instead of driving her home, the man parked the car on an empty street. Pulling out a knife, he held it to her throat. Then he ripped off her panties and raped her. Until that night, she had been a virgin.

"Why did he do it? Why did he do it?" Flo asked Mary and Diane. "I trusted him. I thought he was my friend. Why did he do it?

"He hurt me," she said. If she was depressed about anything more than the rape itself, it was that the rapist blamed the rape on her because of the way she walked and dressed.

When I interviewed Flo in 1975, she said of that time, "I had some pretty blue days. I used to sit and cry to myself, although I can't remember why," as though she had suppressed her memory of the entire event. Her version of events was that when she was sixteen, her brother Cornell made her quit singing so she could concentrate on her schoolwork. "I sat on the porch and cried and cried," Flo said. A short while later, though, according to Flo, she turned seventeen, and her mother told her she had a birthday present for her. "I said, 'What?' [sullenly], because no birthday present interested me at the time. I was just hurt. And she said, 'You can go back and sing.'"

The rape may have been too private for Flo to discuss with me during our interviews, but her niece Katherine (the daughter of Flo's eldest sister) told me flat out that the rapist was the young man who later became the Detroit Pistons center Reginald Harding.

Reginald Harding's life story, from high school talent to early fame to premature death, eerily parallels Florence Ballard's. From his early youth, Harding wanted to be a basketball player. He was certainly built for it. When he entered Eastern High School in Detroit (now Martin Luther King, Jr. High School), he was six feet ten inches. It soon became obvious what he was going to do with his life.

An outstanding center at Eastern, Harding led the team to the Detroit city championship. But always Harding's growing fame and infamy would be mixed together. He was arrested in upstate Michigan in the summer of 1959 for stealing a pickup truck and was sentenced to probation. Then, perhaps more significantly, he was arrested at age eighteen for "carnal knowledge" of a minor in Detroit in 1960, the same year Flo Ballard was raped. The alleged victim was a fifteen-year-old whose first name was Jean, according to court records. At the time of his arrest for statutory rape, Harding was considered the best prep basketball player in the state. He admitted to associating with the girl but denied her charges and was acquitted.

Harding was drafted by the Pistons in 1962 and played spectacularly through 1964, but his career started to falter as he became increasingly engaged in criminal activities. In September 1972, shortly after he was released from Jackson Prison in Michigan after serving a two-year term for probation violation, he was shot by a friend following an altercation in front of an inner-city Detroit house. Harding died of his wounds at Detroit General Hospital. He was thirty years old.

In *The True Story of Florence Ballard*, Flo's sister Maxine Ballard did not explicitly name Reginald Harding as Flo's rapist but hinted at him, stating that the rapist was "well-known (a popular basketball player at the high school)" who was never arrested or tried for the crime. Flo and Maxine's sister Pat said that in 2006 Maxine told her that the rapist was Harding. While none of Flo's relatives would divulge the reason for their certainty, clearly this information could only have come originally from Flo.

Whoever the assailant, Flo would suffer from the rape for the rest of her life. Mary Wilson said that the rape "ate away at Flo's insides. She couldn't handle it. She needed professional help but never got it. She had no counseling and never talked to anyone about it again" after revealing it to Mary and Diane. "She changed from an aggressive person to an angry person. She was scared for the rest of her life, and her life was not nearly as productive" as it would have been otherwise. Nonetheless, Flo returned to the group following the rape, and she and her two remaining partners tapped tall, pretty Barbara Martin, a friend of a friend, as the new fourth Primette.

Trying to jumpstart their careers, the Primettes hung around the lobby at Motown headquarters every day after school, pestering producers, writers, singers—and anyone else who walked by—for the opportunity to record. The only reason they were allowed to stay in the lobby at all was that they were managed on the side by Motown employee Morris, they knew the receptionist, and they flirted with the male Motowners who sauntered by.

Eventually, their pleas were heard, and they were allowed to work as occasional informal backgrounders for big Motown stars such as Marvin Gaye and Marv Johnson. As background singers, the quartet earned $78 a week each. Flo was also babysitting regularly, for $20 a week. "I never even got an allowance at home, maybe a nickel, maybe some bubblegum or a candy bar, but that was it. I felt great when I got the money. The first thing I did was to go home and give my mother some," she said. Mary got a job in a record store. Diane landed a job as Gordy's secretary, which she held for a short while.

This led to a lot of talk, but at this point Diane was more interested in making Gordy pay attention to the group than to her.

Flo's situation started to change. Rarely successful at making her own clothes, Flo was now able to buy some of the clothes she wanted. Her appearance changed too. When she started background singing, she would walk from her home all the way to Motown headquarters, a substantial distance. "Whatever fat I had wasn't there for long after that walk," Flo said. After a while the money and prestige wrought deeper changes. "I began to get my hair curled, whereas before I would just pull it back and that was it. I began to wear more makeup, and I dressed different. I walked better. I was somebody."

The rape may have been a factor in Flo's decision to quit school in the eleventh grade, but she had also founded the Primettes, considered them her group, and was more distracted and consumed by the group than were its other members. Her ability to pay attention at school had suffered in proportion.

Diane, Mary, and Barbara would all graduate, and although Berry Gordy had dropped out, he went on to earn a high school equivalency degree and later razzed Flo about her status as a high school dropout.

Flo's eldest brother, Cornell, was furious when he heard she had dropped out of school. Cornell had taken the role of father in the family when Jesse had died, and Flo was scared of him. "I didn't want to face him, I didn't want to see him," after quitting school, she said. "But he finally caught me."

Cornell grabbed her and said, "I told you to finish school, didn't I?" Flo related.

"I was looking at him and shaking, and I said, 'Well, I done quit now.'"

"I know it," he said. "If Momma had listened to me she wouldn't have let you go on back and sing; you would have finished school."

When Flo's star started to rise, however, Cornell cooled off.

3

Always a Bridesmaid

Flo . . . had the voice we needed.

> —Katherine Anderson Schaffner,
> former Marvelette, speaking of
> Flo's stint with the Marvelettes

THE PRIMETTES SPENT their first year at Motown vocalizing and hand clapping anonymously behind big-name stars. By 1960, though, Gordy could no longer use the excuse that they were still in school to turn aside their pleas to make their own record, since, according to his criteria, they had all "finished" high school. They spent months recording songs that Gordy usually ruled were not worth releasing. Among them was "After All," a tune produced by Smokey Robinson and recorded by the Primettes on October 1, 1960.

Then Motown composer Freddie Gorman, who knew the Primettes from his days as a mail carrier at the Brewster Projects, wrote "I Want a Guy" for Florence and her pals. Gordy recorded this song on the Tamla label, a significant choice for an all-black group in an almost all-black company. He could have dedicated Motown to recording "The Sound of Black America" but chose to call the Motown Sound "The Sound of Young America" instead. The collapse of Gordy's jazz record store had shown him the pitfalls of restricting his audience, and the name "Tamla" symbolized his newfound desire to appeal to whites as well as blacks: it was inspired by the movie *Tammy and the Bachelor*, which starred Gordy's favorite actress, Debbie Reynolds.

Gordy recorded songs on many labels other than Motown and Tamla, including Gordy, Hitsville, Mowest, Rare Earth, Soul, Prodigal, Miracle, and VIP. He was well aware that disc jockeys, often accused of accepting payola from record companies for airing their records, felt more at ease playing records with different label names, even though they knew the labels were produced by one company. Motown may have exceeded any other record company of the era in the number of different labels it slapped on its discs.

The big decision involving "I Want a Guy," however, wasn't in choosing the label under which to produce it; it was in choosing the singer who would sing the lead on it, and Motown executives chose Diane. She also led on the flip-side tune, "Never Again." In spite of awarding her these two leads, Motown executives at the time still saw each member of the group as a possible lead singer, and many were divided over Diane's voice—what some found untrained and thin, others found unique. Flo and Mary were particularly unimpressed. Mary once said, "Whenever Diane would insist on a lead and then sing it, we would sort of look at each other and try not to laugh. She had this weird little whiny sound."

The group certainly didn't hit the big time with this record, which went nowhere. But Flo remained characteristically optimistic, noting that the songs "were both flops, but they were good flops."

Gordy's next move was to assign the group to his top producer, Smokey Robinson, who had come up with instant hits for other early Motown groups. Gordy himself and another company heavy, Barney Ales, Motown's vice president of sales, wrote the raucous dance number "Buttered Popcorn." This time Flo was given the lead—Ales had heard and liked her voice. On the other side was "Who's Loving You?," a version of a Miracles tune.

Before either "I Want a Guy" or "Buttered Popcorn" was pressed and released, Motown execs decided that "Primettes" wouldn't cut it as the group's name—it was too 1950s. The young women themselves were asked to choose a new one from among the many ideas typed out on a sheet of paper, including "The Darleens," "The Sweet Ps," "The Melodees," "The Royaltones," and "The Jew-elettes." Part of the urgency for changing the name was that Gordy now wanted the girls to sign contracts with Motown, and he wanted a group that would keep its moniker, rather than change its name after signing, thereby consigning thousands of dollars of publicity to the ash heap.

The four were given an hour to choose the group's new name. Flo chose "The Supremes" and insisted on it despite opposition from Diane. "I gave us the name 'Supremes,'" Flo said proudly. She saw it as a link with the name "Primettes," which means pretty much the same thing. "Diane said 'No, it sounds like a man's group.' But I bet she's glad to this day that the group was named the Supremes," Flo said.

Actually, two groups had previously used the name "Supremes." One was a male quartet from Columbus, Ohio, which so enjoyed a bottle of Bourbon Supreme that they named themselves after it. They went on to record the song "Just for You and I" as a single on Ace Records. Ruby and the Romantics, who recorded "Our Day Will Come," also had originally called themselves the Supremes. But both groups were out of action, at least under their original names, when Flo chose the name for her group.

Names, as it turned out, were important at Motown, since Gordy managed to keep his hands on many of his groups' names and copyright them. That way, the "groups" could continue to perform for Motown after the individual members had left the company. As a result, many former Motowners would look back mournfully at names that originally had been theirs, watching other singers parade around the country and the world with "hijacked" names while millions cheered.

Once the name issue was settled, Gordy signed Flo, Mary, Diane, and Barbara to their first Motown contract. Because they were minors, their mothers signed for all four of them, on January 15, 1961. None of the mothers or daughters had legal counsel. They all believed Gordy when he said that he and Motown would do only what was best for the young women and that they should allow Motown to completely manage their careers and their money.

In reality, the contract was, as Mary Wilson would put it in 2007, "atrocious." All the money Motown spent on the Supremes would be subtracted from their royalties. In other words, if successful, they would pay for themselves. Although they had formed their own group before Motown existed, if one of them left the group, Motown, not the singers, would select the new group member. The group's records would earn each of them three-fourths of a percent of 90 percent of the suggested retail price for each record, less all taxes and packaging costs. Each would thus receive half a cent from each seventy-five-cent single sold, but all expenses would be taken out first. Under this formula, for each record that sold a million copies, each Supreme would end up receiving five thousand dollars *minus* her share of the cost of all preceding unreleased records by the group as well as her share of all the costs of the record for which she was receiving royalties. While the contract allowed Motown to charge all the expenses of making a Supremes record to the Supremes, it did not require Motown to release any of the group's recordings at all. And Motown became the young women's booking agent, manager, accountant, financial adviser, and lawyer. Each year was divided into two audit periods, and performers were allowed to audit only one of those periods for each year.

Author J. Randy Taraborrelli has argued that despite Motown's boasts, and despite the numerous #1 hits achieved by the Supremes, only two of their records—"Where Did Our Love Go?" and "You Can't Hurry Love"—were instant million-selling records, although the company claimed that the group put out eight million-sellers from 1964 through 1968. Most, perhaps all, of these records later sold a million or more copies in some format, but if you were legally separated from the group, as Flo later was, you would never receive royalties from the sales of any song that occurred after your separation, even if you had participated in recording it and in promoting it through concerts, interviews, and appearances.

Taraborrelli's claim is challenged by those who argue that he may be counting only domestic sales of the records and that Motown's overseas sales were large. The situation is further clouded by the fact that Motown did not join the Recording Industry Association of America (RIAA), which verifies record company sales figures, until 1980. This produces the following conundrum: Did Motown close its books because its "million-selling" singles were not, in fact, selling a million? Or because they were selling a million but they didn't want to pay out a million records' worth of royalties? Or for some other reason?

When you do the math, as the Supremes should have but didn't (although even if they had wanted to, they wouldn't have been able to get a complete picture with the scant information that was released to them), you have to multiply a number that was probably less than one million by the low amounts per record—always less than a cent—awarded the Supremes in their contracts, then subtract their tremendous expenses, and so forth. This doesn't mean that the Supremes who lived long enough and continued to have access to royalties from the following forty-plus years of use of Supreme tunes by private corporations, commercials, Hollywood, Muzak, and so on, didn't eventually become well-off, if not exactly rich.

At the time, however, as far as Motown was concerned, once a Motown song was recorded and earned its first round of income, although it stayed in the company's catalog and was available for sale, it was forgotten. (This attitude extended to photographs of Motown artists, as well. When Motown later left Detroit for Los Angeles, in 1972, it left behind thousands of these photographs. Motown executives believed that the janitors or the new tenants would eventually throw them out, but many of these pictures were liberated by "thieves," "vandals," "collectors," "scholars," "preservationists," "businesspeople," or "dedicated musicologists," depending on your point of view.)

The major problem with the contract the Supremes signed (and with many other record contracts) is that the artists were being charged for expenses over which they had little or no control. Gordy often insisted on very long in-studio recording sessions to get the sound of a Supremes record just right. To be sure, he probably improved the quality of the record by doing so, and that likely improved sales of the record; but all the expenses, including the fee for the studio musicians, were charged to the artists, not to Gordy or Motown.

In defending these contracts, Berry Gordy has put forward several arguments that hold some water: No other record companies developed its artists through an in-house training program to the extent that Motown did. Few record companies kept their artists under contract if they didn't make hits year after year. And few if any other record companies would have kept producing records for a group, like the Supremes, that didn't hit pay dirt until their umpteenth record. Gordy's supporters have also argued that Motown's contracts were no worse than those of many other record companies, at least in the beginning.

While Gordy may have been right about all of the above, the real stingers in the contract were the provisions giving Motown sole control over its artists' money and careers. Motown was unique in not only producing its singers' records but in acting as their lawyer and their agent as well. Everyone worked for Motown, including the attorneys and agents who were supposed to represent the interests of the artists, as opposed to the interests of the record company. Other recording firms allowed artists to hire their own agents and lawyers. Motown did not, at least not in its first few years of operation.

Motown was also, by all accounts, absolutely tenacious in its efforts to keep as much of its artists' money as it possibly could, whether it was entitled to that money or not. Katherine Anderson Schaffner of the Marvelettes said that from the time her group left Motown in 1970, until eighteen years later, in 1988, Motown paid them no royalties whatsoever. When the group sued the company, "They paid us a minimal amount," she said, "and then we had to sue them again" because Motown still was not giving the hit-making Marvelettes everything they were entitled to, even under Motown's stingy contracts.

Whatever the advantages and disadvantages, Motown and the Supremes were now committed partners. And as if by prearrangement, the second record issued under the group's new name began to get some airplay. But only the side on which Flo sang the lead, "Buttered Popcorn," received substantial attention. Flo was still living at home when they played "Buttered Popcorn" on the radio in 1962. "All that day," she said, "I was turning on the radio, turning to different stations, trying to pick it up. It was just a fantastic feeling to hear myself singing. Family members would be calling up and saying, 'I heard you on the radio!' 'I heard you on the radio!' The phone would be jumping off the hook."

If "Buttered Popcorn," a cheery, catchy song with a light and fluffy name, had been promoted into a heavyweight hit, Flo, who sang the lead on the song, might have been locked into that role as the group rose to stardom, with dramatic effect on her career and on those of the other three. Barney Ales wanted to put Motown's publicity machine behind "Buttered Popcorn," but Gordy, who was impressed with Diane's energy and beginning to focus on her rather than on Flo as the potential superstar of the group, wouldn't let Ales promote it. In terms of Florence Ballard's subsequent career, "Buttered Popcorn" may represent the tune not taken, the career that never was. Although relatively unknown these days, except to collectors of rare pop discs, this song is a milestone in the history of Flo Ballard and the Supremes. Later, Gordy also chose not to release another Supremes tune that highlighted Flo's skill as a lead singer, "Save Me a Star."

Mainly owing to a lack of promotion by Motown, "Buttered Popcorn" / "Who's Loving You" didn't do much better than "I Want a Guy." Some of the blame fell justly on producer Smokey Robinson. Robinson had written major hits for other Motown acts, but his genius as a producer was somehow never able to connect with the budding artistic talents of the young Primettes or Supremes. The group's hit tunes, written and produced mostly by others, are easily distinguishable from tunes written and produced by Robinson.

The early demise of "I Want a Guy" and "Buttered Popcorn" signaled the transformation of the Supremes from a quartet into a trio in 1962. Barbara Martin had married and become pregnant, and "Diane thought that was bad for the image," Flo said. "So Barbara left the group because Diane didn't want her in the group." Clearly Diane's power among the Supremes was beginning to manifest itself.

Of course the quartet's downsizing into a trio would turn out not to make a difference. Despite the immense impact of the "Fab Four," many famous groups of the time were in fact trios, including the Andrews Sisters, a group with which the early Supremes were often compared. In any case, what really paved the road to success for the Supremes was the beginning of the "girl group" phenomenon on January 31, 1961, when the Shirelles, a New Jersey quartet, put "Will You Love Me Tomorrow?" at the top of the pop charts, becoming the first all-female pop group of the rock era to do so.

But the three remaining members of the Supremes had other problems. Their continued failure to move forward killed whatever interest Gordy had in them. "The Marvelettes were knocking on the door, and the Vandellas were knocking on the door," Flo said, "and the Marvelettes came right in [one month after the release of "Buttered Popcorn"] and got a smash hit, 'Please Mr. Postman,'" Motown's first #1 Pop hit.

The group's continuing failure to become famous so upset Flo that she temporarily left the Supremes. Rather than stay on the sidelines, she joined the Marvelettes, who were much more successful at the time. Officially, Flo was filling in for Wanda Young, who was pregnant and unable to finish her tour with the Marvelettes in 1962. Flo stayed with the Marvelettes for several months. Mary and Diane were so depressed at the group's lack of popularity and the temporary departure of their leader that they didn't even rehearse, much less perform, while Flo was away.

"Flo fit the bill" for her new venture, former Marvelette Katherine Anderson Schaffner said. "She had the voice we needed." She pointed out, however, that unlike the Primettes or the Supremes, "The Marvelettes liked to dance on stage. We did our own routines." This was hard on Flo: "We laughed because she had a hard time doing the steps. They were foreign to her," Anderson said, "but we told her it was OK. After a while, she did the steps her own way, and we lightened up the steps" to allow Flo to do them more easily.

When Flo finally returned to the Supremes in May 1962, the group went back to performing all around Detroit and also touring sporadically outside the Motor City.

Meanwhile, Hitsville was living up to the hopes Gordy had so fervently invested in it. The big beat in most Motown hits was one reason. Even if Gordy hadn't been intent on producing a big sound, he might have found the development hard to avoid. Motown's first recording studio, a converted room in one of the West Grand Boulevard houses, gave any instrument played in it a big, booming sound. For a while, Gordy thought that this "boom-boom" sound would actually prevent Motown from making good records. But it did just the opposite, appealing to listeners and making Motown's records hard to copy.

While the Supremes couldn't get a hit, they showed spunk by harassing Motown's producers incessantly. "We were still sitting there fussing at the producers," Flo said. "'We were the first group here! And we haven't got a hit record yet!' We wanted a hit so bad we didn't know what to do."

Four other sides written for the group in 1962 and 1963 by Robinson, with Diane as lead, failed to bust the group out of the no-hit ghetto in which they found themselves. The dreamy "Your Heart Belongs to Me" barely pushed its way into the Top 100, and "Let Me Go the Right Way" couldn't move past #90. "My Heart Can't Take It No More" didn't do any better. The wistful "A Breathtaking Guy," originally titled "A Breathtaking, First Sight Soul Shaking, One Night Love Making, Next Day Heartbreaking Guy," made #75, but numbers that low were not going to jumpstart the Supremes' career. They and others noted, however, that their numbers were improving.

During this same period, Motown was producing hits like "Stubborn Kind of Fellow" by Marvin Gaye and "Playboy" by the Marvelettes. In 1962 it produced "Beechwood 4-5789" by the Marvelettes; "The One Who Really Loves You," "You Beat Me to the Punch," and "Two Lovers" by Mary Wells; and "Do You Love Me?" by the Contours. In 1963 it released "You've Really Got a Hold on Me" and "Mickey's Monkey" by the Miracles; "Laughing Boy" by Mary Wells; "Pride and Joy" by Marvin Gaye; "Fingertips—Part 2" by Little Stevie Wonder; and "(Love is Like a) Heat Wave" and "Quicksand" by Martha and the Vandellas. ("Heat Wave" and "Quicksand" are excellent examples of Motown's often successful attempts to produce two songs, and twice the profit, from one. Except for some of the words, the songs were almost identical.)

Flo, Diane, and Mary, on the other hand, were being mocked as the "No-Hit Supremes" by the crueler spirits among their colleagues. Even when they were able to arrange for relatively high-level gigs in Detroit, the freshness of their youth, which many found appealing, hurt them on at least one occasion. A Temptations-Supremes show at Detroit's Twenty Grand Nightclub, a show that Flo called "hot" and "fantastic," lasted for only one week in February 1965 because, while Flo was nearing twenty-two, Diane and Mary were each a month short of twenty-one, the age required for performing in a club with a liquor license.

"The Temptations were dressed in white suits, and we were dressed in white gowns, and at the end of the show we'd do a song together," Flo remembered. "We did the first half of each show, and they did the second because they were a big act and we were nowhere that big."

Then, somehow, the Detroit Police found out what was happening. When the police arrived at the club one night shortly before the performance started, Flo at first thought there was hope for continuing because she had worked as a baby-sitter for one of the children of the lead police officer involved, Doris Jackson. But Officer Jackson could not be moved. "We were pleading with Doris Jackson," Flo said. "We were telling her, 'Well, look, they'll be twenty-one next month,' and she said, 'I can't help it. They're not twenty-one now.'"

The police ordered the Supremes to stop performing halfway through the two-week engagement.

What made the whole scene even more galling for Flo was that "The manager wasn't too upset; the Temptations just kept on anyway—they carried the show on. But we were real hurt, because we wanted to get up there. . . . The next week we just recorded, that was all, no shows. It was embarrassing."

But that November, the young women piled into a bus and five cars with many other Motown acts to tour much of America as the Motortown Revue.

4

Roughing It

*They didn't serve black people in the front. . . . You
don't come in; they give you your food to take with
you. . . . You better carry it out, or you get shot.*

—Florence Ballard, remembering
the Motortown Revue Tour

THE MOTORTOWN REVUES were unique to Motown. No other record company had found it necessary or desirable to send all its artists on tour together.
But because Motown was not only a struggling young company but also a
company with many all-black acts, Gordy worried that sending each act out
on its own might be financial suicide.

The fact was that the big talent agencies that arranged concert tours in
the early 1960s weren't very interested in dealing with black acts at all, and
certainly not with one black act at a time. When Motown put all its acts
together, however, the package involved so much potential profit for the
agents that even the most prejudiced among them were willing to book the
Motortown Revues into clubs and theaters.

The Motortown Revues were massive. The 1962 Revue that Flo and the
other Supremes joined included forty-five performers. "It was too many people
and too many miles and showed a lack of experience putting all those people

out there," the Motown executive who managed that tour said. But the Revues introduced a lot of Motown acts to a lot of fans.

And what an introduction. As *Rolling Stone* noted later, "There'd be the bongos, and Little Stevie Wonder would come on and open the show; and then it would go on nonstop with the Marvelettes and the Contours—who had 'Do You Love Me?'—and Mary Wells and the Temptations and all the others and wind up with Smokey Robinson and the Miracles. Stevie'd do that showstopper where he'd get down on one knee and then flat on the floor, singing 'a little bit softer now . . . a little bit softer now' right down to where he was hardly whispering, and then he'd start to crank it up 'a little bit louder now . . . a little bit louder now . . .' until he was back up jumping and pumping full steam and the roof would fall in."

The Revues served other functions: eliminating the acts that couldn't cut it and illuminating the superstars in the group. In this sense, they operated very much like farm teams in baseball. Sometimes the touring artists weren't as well prepared as they might have been. Occasionally, performers would have only a day or two to learn a whole new act, or they'd have to wear hand-me-down costumes that were too tight and came apart at embarrassing moments.

For the performers who were high school dropouts living in housing projects when they joined Motown, for those who'd rarely been beyond the Detroit city limits, for those who had been born in the North and had never been in the South, traveling around America, even by bus, was a thrilling yet shocking experience. As for Flo, the Motortown Revue took her to the South for the first time and showed her the ugly face of true segregation.

But the Motortown Revues were above all grueling. Sometimes they involved six shows a day and seventeen one-nighters in a row. On November 2, 1962, the artists performed in Boston; on November 3 in New Haven; the next day, in Buffalo; and on the next days in Raleigh; Charleston; Augusta; Savannah; Birmingham; Columbus, Georgia; Atlanta; Mobile; New Orleans; Jackson; Spartanburg, South Carolina; Durham, North Carolina; Columbia, South Carolina; and Washington, D.C. Then the groups got a day off.

Flo and her fellow Supremes never received any money above expenses for their work on the Motortown Revue, and the young women certainly weren't dressed elaborately for the tour. For the one or two numbers the Supremes performed, "all we had was about three or four changes, which were just plain cotton suits," Florence said. "Suits we paid $20, maybe $25 apiece for. Shirt and top or skirt and jacket. One dress we had, it was a white dress; it was a nice dress, summer dress, cotton, think we paid about $10 apiece for it. Oh boy," she said sarcastically, "those were the days."

All the groups were together on one bus and its trailing cars: among them Mary Wells, Smokey Robinson and the Miracles, twelve-year-old Stevie Wonder, and, basically just along for the ride, the Supremes. The lifestyle was communal beyond belief. This led, naturally, to romantic entanglements. Flo and Otis Williams of the Temptations were one such short-lived item.

The rigors of the Revue had its rewards, in the form of audiences eager for the groups that had already produced hit records. When the master of ceremonies introduced the Marvelettes, the audience, hooked on the group's million-seller, "Please Mr. Postman," went into hysterics. The Marvelettes' name was prominent on the marquee. By contrast, the Supremes' name was often unlisted altogether. The Supremes were frequently the first group or among the first groups to perform, giving them the status of a warm-up act rather than a "featured" act. Those preferred acts were introduced later, after the warm-up groups had prepped the audience.

Even under the stress of endless days on a bus, and the ego-reducing effects of performing for people who had never heard of her, Flo's confidence remained undimmed. Only a small portion of the audience recognized any song the Supremes might perform, including "Who's Loving You?" the flip side of "Buttered Popcorn," but Flo continued to urge the group to put all its energy into each and every performance.

"We had records out; they just weren't hits," Flo said. "But regardless of that, we still went over. I think it was the way we carried ourselves, plus our good looks; plus we had talent. Maybe not a hit record, but we had talent, that's for sure." While Diane was in tears about the Supremes' reception at the Apollo, which seemed to her to consist of merely polite applause, Flo saw the glass as half-full. "We didn't have a hit when we were at the Apollo, but we still went over; we went over great," Flo said.

Compared with the Marvelettes, "We were a better group," Flo said. "We had better harmony." She argued that "the Marvelettes couldn't sing, not really." She dismissed the Contours as "a screaming act. They could sing, but they needed material, and I don't think too many producers wanted to write for them. . . . I don't know what happened to them. One of them became a junkie. Some of them went into factories to work and just gave it up." Flo never stopped criticizing the other groups—although never to their faces—as well as boosting her own. But she was also realistic enough to admit that the Supremes badly needed a hit.

Whatever the varying abilities of the groups involved, on this tour they were all black and all together in the segregated South. "We were in Macon, Georgia, doing one-nighters," Flo remembered. "We had finished the show, and we were all getting on the bus. It was pitch black. . . . Mary Wells was getting on the bus, and we hear something say, 'Pow!'—like that. We said, 'That might be a firecracker. Who's popping firecrackers?' Then all of a sudden the bus driver says, 'Hey, everybody hit the floor, quick!' Somebody was shooting at us. Why? Because we was black! A bus full of black artists. The only white one on the bus was the bus driver, and he was scared. No one was hit. So we got to Fort Lauderdale, Florida, that morning; we were all asleep on the bus. The bus driver got off, and he happened to be walking and he looked at the front of the bus, bullet holes was all in the front of the bus. He woke us up and he said, 'Look! Told you those was bullets!' Somebody could have got hit."

Although the tours played to mixed audiences—a harbinger of Motown's future success in a world in which whites were the major record buyers—the white and black people in the audience were never allowed to mingle. Either the blacks were required to sit upstairs and the whites downstairs or the blacks had to sit on one side of the theater and the whites on the other. Restrooms were segregated by color as well as gender.

In fact, finding restrooms they could use was a continuing and annoying problem. The members of the Miracles "went up to a gas station and asked the guy could they use the bathroom," Florence remembered. He said, 'Hell, no,' and got a shotgun out. And all of them came flying back to the bus. So we had to get in a deep, dark spot and the girls took their turn in the back of the bus, and then the guys took their turn in the back of the bus, because there was nowhere to stop."

Restaurants were also a major problem. If the touring artists couldn't find a blacks-only restaurant on a particular day, they were out of luck. They sometimes tried to make light of it. Comedian Bill Murray would occasionally go up to a whites-only restaurant and try to order a sandwich. When the expected response was uttered—"We don't serve black people"—he'd retort with "I don't eat 'em either."

Apart from suffering from segregationist laws in the South, some Motown performers had occasional similar problems even in the North. A white Motown public relations employee, Alan Abrams, often accompanied Smokey Robinson and the other Miracles on tour. Abrams and the group would usually stay in the same hotel. On one tour, though, when the group was performing in Chicago, Abrams arrived late and took a room by himself in a Hyde Park hotel. Robinson dropped over to talk to him. After Robinson left, the hotel manager called Abrams and told him he'd have to leave the hotel because it was against the rules to have black visitors.

In the South the Motown performers were barnstorming through a largely segregated area at a time when civil rights leaders were fighting to have equal rights for blacks made law, when civil rights marchers were met with police dogs and fire hoses, and when troops were needed to force the admission of black students to southern high schools and universities. The Motown performers tried to figure out far in advance what hotels would house them and what restaurants would feed them. But their day might begin with a visit to a restaurant where they would be refused service in the front. "They didn't serve black people in the front," Florence recalled. "They've got a little place around the back; you go around in the back, and they've got a window. You don't come in; they give you your food to take with you. . . . You better carry it out, or you get shot!"

In Miami Beach, as the Motortown Revue acts were checking into a motel, fifteen police cruisers with dogs pulled up outside and waited as the performers entered the motel. When they left later in the day to perform, the cruisers were still there. Finally, someone went out and explained to the cops that this was a musical show on tour, and the surveillance was finally lifted.

Flo and the others were often shocked by the squalor they were forced to endure. "The hotels we stayed in were unbelievable. Bad," she said. "But you know I would like to go back just to see the changes. . . . [Then it was all] roaches, broken-down facilities, bad plumbing, face bowls and stuff; some of them didn't even have bathtubs. You know, like a flophouse. But you're black—you've got to stay there."

Nevertheless, especially in the North, the Motortown Revues often attracted large, somewhat integrated, and entirely peaceful crowds. "We were the only whites there," said Nancy Van Goethem, who attended one show in Detroit, "but there was no fear in us. Maybe we were naive girls from the suburbs, but there was such a feeling of camaraderie and togetherness. Everyone would be on their feet, moving their bodies as much as they could, dancing in front of their seats."

The Motortown Revues would eventually be disbanded, but only because individual Motown artists would become so well known that they could draw large crowds touring on their own.

After the 1962 Motortown Revue, the Supremes, still without a hit record, languished in the record-biz equivalent of a segregated rooming house. It's hard to imagine what not having a hit meant at Motown in terms of the pecking order, but one clue is that at a Motown Christmas party held in the

Supremes' early days, they received tiny transistor radios as Christmas presents. The hit-making Marvelettes received diamond rings.

Still, Gordy was impressed by the professionalism the Supremes displayed. Undaunted by their string of duds, they continued to perform as background singers, tour, and make local appearances into 1964. Also, Gordy hadn't worked in a factory for nothing: he knew the value of interchangeable parts. The way he arranged things at Motown, nothing tied any particular artist or group at the company to any particular producer or writer, unless they began making hits together. In fact, writers, producers, and artists were like the hands of a clock, constantly revolving—sometimes together, sometimes apart.

Sometimes, the tracks that were recorded revolved rather than the groups themselves. The Supremes, for instance, recorded many tracks that were never finished and that are still sitting in Universal Music / Motown's vault waiting to be overdubbed. In fact, in 1975, reacting to an epidemic of discomania, Motown released an album called *The Magic Disco Machine*, which consisted entirely of old background tracks never fitted to lead parts.

If a song didn't work for the Supremes, it might work for the Vandellas or the Marvelettes. The company would lay different voices over the same background track and see what happened. Writers and producers also were interchanged, rotated from group to group as the company searched for better combinations. Gears revolved within gears. Producers would rotate from song to song on a single album recorded by a single group. As many as twelve different producers would produce songs on the same album, causing one critic to call some Motown albums "musical quilts." If a group didn't create a hit with one producer, it would be moved on to another producer, and then to another.

Artists also climbed aboard the mechanical merry-go-round. Different artists performed together at different times or on different albums. These constant revolutions were necessary because Motown's products were not always perfect. Brenda Holloway wrote a song for the Supremes that she was going to call "You Don't Hold Me in Your Arms the Way You Did," but someone goofed. On the master record, the background singing and music, which sounded like "bah-bah-bah," was much louder than the lead tune the Supremes were singing. Motown would release it anyway, on the Supremes' *Reflections* album, under the title "Bah-Bah-Bah."

When a superb combination was found, however, the gears stopped revolving a while. So, when the Supremes were finally assigned to the song-writing team of Lamont Dozier and the brothers Eddie and Brian Holland, known within the company and eventually throughout music world as "Holland-Dozier-Holland" (H-D-H), the gears stopped, and real time began.

5

"Boom-Boom-Boom-Boom, Boom-Boom-Boom-Boom, Ba-by, Ba-by"

The song was different, simple, and had good timing.

—Flo Ballard, on "Where Did Our Love Go?"

EDDIE HOLLAND WAS best known for his lyrics, his younger brother Brian for his engineering and production skills, and Lamont Dozier for his melodies. The Supremes' first single with H-D-H, "When the Lovelight Starts Shining Through His Eyes," climbed into the Top 40, peaking at #23 on the *Billboard* charts in the fall of 1963. Heavy on saxes and tambourines, rhythm, and melody, it was a harbinger of hits to come. The flip side of this record, "Standing at the Crossroads of Love," was reworked three years later and became "Standing in the Shadows of Love," which, as recorded by the Four

Tops, reached #6 on the Pop charts. Apparently not recognizing either tune's potential, H-D-H next foisted the bland "Run, Run, Run" on the Supremes and watched the song nearly fall off a cliff (it barely clung to the #100 mark).

In the spring of 1964, however, H-D-H wrote "Where Did Our Love Go?" When they brought it to Gordy, he suggested it for the Marvelettes, but they turned it down. It was then offered to the Supremes. Their unanimous reaction: forget it. Flo remembered, "We said, 'Huh, we don't like this record. It don't sound like nothing to us.' We wanted something like 'Please Mr. Postman,'" which they were well aware had reached #1 almost instantly in 1961.

"Where Did Our Love Go?" was the best and earliest example of what came to be called the Motown Sound, a sound that stemmed from Gordy's ancestral roots in Africa and Georgia and his life in mechanized Detroit. The beat was all-important; all else was built upon it. This heavy beat was a natural connection between the African past and the mechanized present. Motown itself called the Motown Sound "a stylized reflection of African-American tradition," and that's what it was: African American tradition updated by the incessant pounding of the punch press and buffed to a shiny gloss by contact with an urban society.

But more than that, it sold records. "Rhythm is basic," Gordy said. "If you get that, that's what people want." He invited local kids to drop by and evaluate early Motown songs. He learned that they wanted something to dance to, so the beat came first and the lyrics second. Gordy listened to what they said. Characteristically, once convinced that a strong, accentuated beat would be accepted, he took no half measures. He added rhythmic hand clapping, a repetitive chorus, and jangling tambourines to the pounding drums, giving Motown's records a unique drive. This heavy but happy beat not only made Motown's records good to dance to, it also forced the company's music into the ear, making Motown's music highly contagious and instantly recognizable. You could literally hear hits coming. Millions of people would soon anticipate "Where Did Our Love Go?" the moment they heard, "Boom-boom-boom-boom, boom-boom-boom-boom, Ba-by Ba-by." *Rolling Stone* wrote that "the sound mixes with your bloodstream and heartbeat even before you begin to listen to it."

Motown producers argued over which Supreme should have the lead on this one. Few people in Detroit or at Motown at the time believed Diane to be a very good singer. When she had started working as a secretary at Motown, other employees called her "a secretary who thought she could sing." People outside the company also criticized her vocal skills. For example, reviewer Alan Betrock later noted that "on recording after recording on their first album, *Meet the Supremes*, Ross is noteworthy only for her inability to stay on key."

Despite these assessments, the producers decided on Diane to sing lead on "Where Did Our Love Go?" Her sound, they said, was unique. Besides, Ross had other qualities that impressed Gordy, traits that he shared himself—ambition, talent, a strong work ethic, a love of competition, and a burning desire to win. When the Supremes were still unknown and were the warm-up act rather than the featured act in the Motown Revue, Ross would sit in the audience the day before and watch what all the other acts did. Then she'd imitate them before they appeared. The other performers complained that they looked ridiculous and imitative when they finally got out on stage, but Gordy so admired her determination that, rather than tell Ross to stop, he told the other artists to alter their routines.

And Ross, in turn, admired Gordy. While Flo had the talent to be the lead singer of the Supremes, she was self-contained and remained aloof from Gordy. Diane was just the opposite. From the very first day she met Berry Gordy, she admired him, flirted with him, catered to him, and strove to impress him. She succeeded, and eventually the two would fall in love. Starting in 1965, they would become romantically involved, and although they would both go on to marry several times to other people over the years, they would carry on a long romantic relationship and, after that, a friendship throughout their lives.

Shortly after "Where Did Our Love Go?" was recorded, Motown persuaded Dick Clark, the host of the popular television program *American Bandstand*, to include the Supremes in his summer of 1964 "Caravan of Stars" tour of the United States. They persuaded him partly by agreeing to send the Supremes on the thirty-six-day tour for a total cost to Clark of $600 a week. Although the young women were all in their early twenties now, Diane's mother was sent along as chaperone. That meant the Supremes and Mrs. Ross were earning $150 a week apiece on the road. Even in the 1960s, that wasn't much to write home about, especially when the group's expenses were deducted from it. But Motown execs made it clear to the Supremes that they were doing them a favor by including them on such a prestigious tour. The ads for the tour, which began in June 1964, highlighted "Gene Pitney! The Shirelles! Brenda Holloway! And Others!" Gordy's sister Esther Edwards, who worked at Motown, made it explicit. She told the Supremes that the company had had to beg Clark to include them in the tour group and that they were really along only for filler. (Later, Gordy would reverse the bargaining field with Clark, saying he would *allow* Clark to have the Supremes only if Clark agreed to take along another Motown group still trying to make it.) The Supremes, especially after Esther Edwards's pep talk, assumed the Dick Clark tour would be just another tour. "Thirty days on a bus. Good grief," Flo said.

Acts such as Bob B. Soxx and the Blue Jeans, and Bobbie Freeman were part of the tour and on the bus with the Supremes. And mashed in with the vocalists was the band, mostly older guys who knew how to party. "You'd try to sleep, and they'd get happy blowing their horns in your ear," Flo said, "but after a while you'd get so tired you'd get on the bus and—I don't care how much noise they were making—you'd go to sleep; you'd just go to sleep."

She had a lot to sleep through. This was the tour on which Diane began showing her royal side. According to accounts from her fellow bus passengers over the years, including Mary Wilson, Diane fought bitterly with other female vocalists over such items as hairspray, the borrowing of a pair of shoes, and the use of the mirror in the bus's one bathroom. Diane clearly believed that she was always right and that anyone who clashed with her was always wrong. Her behavior got her kicked off the bus several times, but she always managed to sweet-talk her way back on.

Between the lack of suitable integrated motels and the fact that a busload of people shared one bathroom, it was difficult for any of the women to style or even wash their hair. Their only fallback was to wear wigs, which grew in number, size, and complexity almost every day. The Supremes' wigs became fetishes, with Diane's the most extravagant of all. Her eventual crowning glory was a wig modeled after the hairstyle worn by former Mouseketeer and beach-movie icon Annette Funicello. Diane combined Funicello's hairstyle with the makeup style of the superthin, "It" model of the day, Twiggy, to create a new look for many women and certainly a new look for black women. Of course the slender Diane *could* be a black Twiggy; Flo definitely could not.

When the tour began, the Supremes were again the lowly opening act, and the applause they received was unimpressive. By contrast, Flo noted, when the master of ceremonies mentioned the Marvelettes' name, "the audience just flipped out." The Supremes were performing gamely, even under such conditions, when they began to notice that something was up. It turned out to be them. The MC kept calling on the group later and later in the show, the applause increased in volume, and the crowds at each stop acted differently.

"They'd just mention our name before we'd walk out on stage, and people would start going mad," Flo said. The three women soon found out why. "Where Did Our Love Go?" had rocketed to #1 on the charts. It was to stay there for eleven weeks.

"The song was different, simple, and had good timing," Flo remarked, having revised her opinion after the song took off. "People started going crazy over us." As often as they could, the three women would rush to buy *Billboard* or *Cashbox* to see how far up the charts their first hit had climbed.

Although some in the company were still rooting for Flo as the lead Supreme, "Where Did Our Love Go?" would help cement that job for Diane. The song, which began with the memorable hammered-out phrase "Ba-by,

Ba-by," was written to be sung by a girlish type, and that was Diane to a T. Small and delicate, with big, wide eyes and a high-pitched voice, she was perfect as the lead singer on a song that pleaded flirtatiously with the dominant male to whom it was addressed. Flo—tall, voluptuous, and deep-voiced—wasn't built for the part. She was also a strong and independent woman, very much like Motown stars Martha Reeves and Mary Wells, both of whom would later leave the company.

As "Where Did Our Love Go?" shot skyward on the charts, Gordy called the Supremes and told them to fly home from California rather than take the bus. It was the first plane ride any of them had ever taken, and they shortly discovered they would be catching planes almost every day after that for months on end. Their climb had begun.

Flo remarked, "I really liked catching a plane because my back was killing me, and my seat was swelling on all those buses." She also noted, "Thirty days of that can kill you. It can. It can."

After their return from the tour, the Supremes were told that travel expenses had eaten up more than their earnings. The cost of publicity, second-rate motel rooms, and carry-out meals aside, Motown paid the women who'd just hit #1 nothing for their three months on the bus tour.

6

In Pursuit of False Gods

*A hell of a singer, probably the strongest of the
three girls.*

—Marvin Gaye, on Florence Ballard

BERRY GORDY congratulated Flo, Mary, and Diane with unusual warmth when they returned to Detroit from the Dick Clark tour. No longer were they the "No-Hit Supremes." "Where Did Our Love Go?" had turned them into the "Group with a Future." But the Supremes were hardly alone in producing a hit for Motown that year. Others included "The Way You Do the Things You Do" by the Temptations, "You're a Wonderful One" by Marvin Gaye (with strong backing vocals by Flo), and "My Guy" by Mary Wells. "After a while it was like Dial-a-Hit," says a former Motown songwriter. "Just like dialing the fire department."

But Flo, Mary, and Diane had definitely become stars, and underneath all their excited and self-congratulatory thoughts lurked the terrible twin questions: Can we stay on the fast track to fame and fortune? and Will Diane sing lead on every song?

Their first priority was to get their act into tip-top shape. The second was to play the major venues worldwide and be dazzlingly successful at them. The third was to fight it out for group dominance. The first step took place in private, the second in front of millions, and the third, behind closed doors.

Although it may seem odd now to think of Florence Ballard as the potential leader of a group that later became Diana Ross and the Supremes, it was anything but odd when the group began its climb. Marvin Gaye saw Flo as "a hell of a singer, probably the strongest of the three girls."

This strong singer was now part of a hit-making group in training. Maurice King, who reigned as Motown's Artist Development maestro, taught them their singing parts for each new song. (The parts were different for each woman, since they were performing in three-part harmony.) King and Motown choreographer Cholly Atkins mapped out their stage act down to the last hand gesture.

Atkins had had a lot of experience mapping out stage acts. Born Charles Atkinson, he had won a dance contest early in life and gone on to a long career in show business. In 1946, he and Charles "Honi" Coles formed the team of Coles and Atkins. They toured with the Count Basie, Cab Calloway, and Lionel Hampton bands. Later on, Atkins choreographed Little Anthony and the Imperials, Frankie Lymon and the Teenagers, the Cadillacs, the Cleftones, Gladys Knight and the Pips, and the Moonglows. Where Cholly was, choreography followed.

King and Atkins concentrated mostly on Mary and Flo, not because they were any less skilled than Diane but because Diane, who had most of the leads, had more freedom to move on her own, whereas Mary and Flo performed strictly choreographed routines that kept them behind their mikes. This rankled. Modeling teacher Maxine Powell taught manners and techniques to all three Supremes. It wasn't easy to climb out of the back seat of a limo or up onto a piano wearing a miniskirt and retain any dignity.

Since the Supremes had had only one hit so far and their tunes before that had been less than memorable, they learned a raft of standard tunes, such as "Put on a Happy Face" and "The Girl from Ipanema." Their plan was to mix these standards in with their one hit and what they hoped would be their future hits. All that mixing, however, required them to rush into the recording studio as soon as they returned from the road, record a tune that had been prepared for them while they were away, and then rush back out on tour, hoping the song they had just recorded would rise to the top of the charts while they were out performing. If it did, they would then be able to sing it live for the first time to an audience that would by then be demanding its performance.

There was no question that the Motown spotlight was now on the Supremes. Gordy kept urging his producers to make their best efforts for the group, yet for a while none of the songs they recorded during these brief breaks between nightclub engagements managed to rise to #1. Still, Gordy was optimistic about the Supremes' prospects and sent them, along with many other Motown acts, to tour England in October 1964. This tour was much different for Flo and her friends than the domestic Motortown Revue Tours, on which they had been hangers-on at best. This time, they were the stars.

Gordy was optimistic about Motown's prospects in Europe. For years, white English groups had been covering and rerecording black music for the English market. Gordy had a hunch that English buyers would be interested in the real thing if they were exposed to it. The company's English contacts weren't encouraging, however. English record retailers had told Motown executives that there were too many tambourines on the company's records and that English record buyers didn't like tambourines.

There was another potential problem. The established English radio stations looked down their noses at black records and often refused to play them. But pitching and rolling in the icy waters just outside British territorial limits were modern-day pirate ships, seaborne radio stations broadcasting illegally into England. The pirates were determined to show their power by making hits out of records the legal stations wouldn't even play. With pirate support, the Supremes, at least, were successful.

The ground for their arrival had been well prepared. Growing prosperity and parental permissiveness in 1950s England had allowed groups of mostly young white men to dress sharp, hang out at clubs all night, and use amphetamines. Called "Mods," short for "Moderns," they were intent on being fashionable and discerning not only in their choice of clothing but also of music.

Since British pop charts at the time were dominated by white hits, the Mods reacted by becoming major fans of rhythm and blues, produced mostly by black Americans, and quickly jumped on the Motown bandwagon.

The Supremes started out the tour riding English buses between engagements, "and their buses are even worse, I mean really worse" than American buses, Florence noted. "But eventually we were able to get a limousine, which we got because we were making big money there. . . . It was really a ball over there, except I couldn't get used to the food. . . . But the people were just fantastic. They were just all around the airport with so many beautiful flowers."

While the group was touring England, "Baby Love," which they'd recorded over the summer, started climbing the charts, hitting #1 on October 25, 1964. In fact, life in Europe got better and better as time went on. "Other than the food, Europe was a ball," Flo said. "One thing I liked there was the clothes, the way they dressed over there. . . . I like the discotheques there, the places to go. And they had lots of places to go for entertainment.

"There's a guy in the Animals who wanted to take me out one night. I think he came up to my shoulder (in height), and I said, 'Oh no, that would never do.' But we all left and got together at the disco and danced and had a ball, let our hair down, then went back to the hotel, went to sleep, got up. . . . It was relaxing to go to the discos and get away from our work. It was relaxing to sit back and watch somebody else work, to sit around, listen to music, drink, have a dance, unwind."

The Supremes were on a fast path to the top, and the three women were still, at this point, clearly able to enjoy spending time together.

7

Supremes at the Summit

*I said, 'Oh wow! The Beatles want to meet us.
We must really be somebody!'*

—Florence Ballard

ONCE BACK IN the states, the Supremes wouldn't get much chance for another rest break. "We began to do a lot of TV work," Flo said. "*Ed Sullivan, Hollywood Palace*, places like that. . . . After people see you on TV, nightclub owners and like that, then they'll start hiring you. And the offers began to roll in; boy, did they roll in . . . the Copacabana, Coconut Grove . . ."

The Supremes' popularity grew, as Flo noted, as a result of their repeat appearances on national television programs. They were the guests of Steve Allen, Red Skelton, and Dean Martin, the TV icons of their time. But most important of all was *The Ed Sullivan Show*, at the time an unprecedented maker or breaker of pop acts.

A former reporter for the New York *Daily News*, Ed Sullivan wasn't handsome; he bent too far forward, held his hands together either behind or in front of him or stood on stage with his arms folded, pronounced "show" as "shew," blew his lines regularly, and often mumbled incoherently. But TV was so new and insecure at the time that CBS executives decided that a man such as Sullivan, credentialed by the New York *Daily News*—an obviously solid social institution—and a former MC of some war relief performances during

World War II, had the best shot at winning audience acceptance for their national variety show. The show was a major success. At eight o'clock every Sunday night, millions of people gathered round their TV sets to watch and listen to the entertainers Sullivan had chosen for them. He introduced more than ten thousand musical and performing acts and artists to the American people from 1948 through 1971. Sullivan was the star maker of the age.

The Supremes' first appearance on *The Ed Sullivan Show* on December 27, 1964, was a nail-biter. "The first time we did the Sullivan show we almost didn't get on," Flo said. "There was something about his show, they say it's always best to be second or third on his show because if for some reason the show runs over, and you're the last one on, you won't get on, you won't get on at all. [On that first show] we almost didn't make it. We were supposed to do two tunes, but we could only do one. After that, we began to be pushed up to the front of the show."

Those who see videotapes of *The Ed Sullivan Show* will find themselves amazed all over again at the changes in show business since the 1960s. *The Ed Sullivan Show* was America's major national television show, yet the Supremes were backed on stage with what looked like a large piece of white paper, and they were fronted with one lone microphone on a stand, into which all of them attempted to sing.

Nevertheless, the Supremes' appearance on the show, singing their third consecutive #1 hit, "Come See About Me," was a major step for the three women. Before this point, they had been intruders in the vast, white, middle-class culture that governed American acceptance. The show cemented their national and cross-cultural appeal, and they were invited back many times.

"We appeared on his show so many times," Flo said. "He got to know us then, and it got to the point where after we would finish doing a number, he would come over and talk to us. That's when we knew we were stars. . . . We became very close to Ed Sullivan, and a lot of people used to ask me, 'Well, how is he? Is he mean?' and I said, 'No, he's a very, very nice man; he's very sweet to me.' He talked backstage with the same voice that he talked with out front. That's his natural thing."

The Supremes also knew they had arrived when the Coca-Cola Company hired them to do commercials for its soft drinks in May 1965. That same month they did a ten-day stint in Atlantic City, New Jersey, where Flo was impressed by the sheer volume of the money changing hands. "In those ten days we grossed over $100,000. Boy, I sure wish I could have gotten my hands on it."

But perhaps the pinnacle of the Supremes' popularity occurred in August of that year, when the Mission Control Center of the National Aeronautics and Space Administration (NASA) in Houston played "Where Did Our Love Go?" for the *Gemini 5* astronauts who were then orbiting the earth. Those now jaded by the space shuttle's comings and goings cannot grasp what awe the astronauts inspired in the 1960s. For the Supremes, having one of their songs beamed to *Gemini 5* astronauts, who were at the center of the world's attention that day, was an honor of the highest order.

After this year of unprecedented success for the Supremes, Berry Gordy had the three women, none of whom was represented by a lawyer, sign a new contract with Motown—a contract so one-sided that it became the model for all future Motown contracts. As under the previous contract, which the Supremes' mothers had signed several years earlier, Motown would continue to keep complete control of the Supremes' name, no matter who recorded under that name. If one Supreme was absent at a particular recording session and a substitute stood in for her, Motown would still call the resulting record a Supremes record but the absent Supreme would receive no royalties. Nothing in the contract required the company to make any recording of any songs sung by the women. If Motown allowed them to sit in the Motown building silently year after year, they'd sit there unpaid year after year. And if the company lost money on any particular recording, the contract allowed Motown to take it from any money the women might earn through live performances or other musical endeavors.

In contrast to the previous contract, however, this new contract gave each member of the group 8 percent of 90 percent, a substantial raise from the three-fourths of one percent of 90 percent that they were receiving previously. But this time, the percentages were applied to the wholesale price of the record, not its recommended retail price, as in the previous contract. The wholesale price was half the retail price. In other words, they were hogtied.

White record owners had taken advantage of black artists for years. Now Flo saw Gordy following in their footsteps. As she later remarked, "I'm telling you, the way Motown did some of those artists was a shame. We were just working, and Berry Gordy was the pimp; and we was like whatever you want to call it, we were making the money, and he was the only one prospering, not the artist."

But these thoughts came later. At the time, Flo saw mostly good in Gordy. She said she had "so much riding on him, faith, trust." "I respected the guy for what he was. He would tell me, 'Your money is being invested in stock, whatever; your money is in an account,' with his signature on it and mine. He couldn't draw without my signature; I couldn't draw without his signature. Where the account went, I don't know. Where the stock went, I don't know."

Aside from this invested money, Flo and the other women would each receive a weekly allowance that would rise under the new contract from $50 a week each to $225 a week. As they had under their previous contract, the Supremes' bank accounts grew, but slowly, since Motown continued to deduct from their royalties all the expenses of recording and producing their records, as well as the costs of sending them around the country and the world on tour.

As the number of their hits increased, the Supremes continued recording. They would record albums that included their own previous hits just before recording their next hoped-for hit. They'd also record at least two albums a year and 45s of all types—anything at all, in fact, to keep the "Supremes" name in front of the public and ratchet up their revenues. This output included the albums *A Bit of Liverpool, The Supremes Sing Country and Western and Pop, Merry Christmas, We Remember Sam Cooke*, and *Supremes at the Copa*—in 1964 and 1965 alone.

Beyond television and recording, the Supremes' nightclub performances were the centerpiece of their fame, especially their appearances at the Copacabana in New York City, where they debuted in July 1965. The Copa was home to the major superstars of the time, such as Sammy Davis Jr., Frank Sinatra, and Tony Bennett. It was also the de facto gatekeeper for all the other upper-echelon nightclubs. As they say about New York itself, if you could make it at the Copa, you could make it anywhere.

Playing at the Copa, which served a largely white, well-heeled audience, meshed perfectly with Gordy's crossover ambitions. To build the Supremes' cross-racial appeal, he had them perform their latest hits interspersed with tunes from the likes of Cole Porter and Stephen Sondheim. The Supremes started the show on July 29, 1965, with "From This Moment On." They then segued into "Put on a Happy Face," performed three of their own hits, and went right into "Rock-a-Bye Your Baby with a Dixie Melody." After that they sang a female version of "King of the Road" called "Queen of the House," performed "Somewhere" from *West Side Story*, and finished with "You're Nobody 'til Somebody Loves You." Not exactly a black-power set.

In all fairness, however, Gordy had chosen exactly the right mix for the Copa, and the Supremes' appearance there was a massive success. Their triumph was partly due to the fact that something about the group's elegant, feminine look fit the Copa aesthetic and the upper-crust circuit perfectly. In October 1965, after their Copa triumph, the Supremes would perform at Philharmonic Hall to a standing-room-only crowd.

By contrast, other Motown acts—Marvin Gaye, Smokey Robinson and the Miracles, and the Four Tops—all flopped at the Copa. It would be tempting to say that Copa audiences were partial to Motown women and less inclined to applaud Motown men, but the Temptations also did very well there—after an unnerving incident recounted in *The Temptations* by Otis

Williams. Group member Melvin Franklin, who, like all the other Tempts, was wearing smooth-soled dancing shoes, tripped on some stray beads from a Copa Girl's costume and spread-eagled himself all over the stage during a typical Tempts trot and twist. He recovered.

All three Supremes were ecstatic about the thunderous applause they received at the Copa and subsequently at other four-star nightclubs, although some aspects of playing the big clubs surprised Flo. "At all the clubs we were treated very well, very respectable," she said. "Copacabana [owner] Jules Podell, he's dead now, fantastic guy, anything we wanted, we got it. The audience was great, but it's like the audience was sitting here and you're right up there singing. They're sitting right up on you. There's no stage, the stage was just the floor, and that took some getting used to. All the tables are sitting on the floor, and you're on the floor also. But you can see very well. And at the Copa they have those girls come out first and dance, just like in the Pearl Bailey era."

One 1965 performance at the Copa became the occasion for a historic meeting between the world's two most popular singing groups, the Supremes and the Beatles.

"We were playing the Copa and they were playing somewhere in New York," Flo said. "They had their manager call the Copa and say they wanted to meet us. And I said, 'Oh wow! The Beatles want to meet us. We must really be somebody!"

By then the Supremes really *were* somebody, but the Beatles didn't know what to make of them. The difference between reality and expectation on both sides was heightened by the fact that the Beatles were under siege and not at their best. Because the adulation to which they were subjected had become uncontrollable and dangerous, it had been decided to make this their last public tour. Lodged at the Warwick in Manhattan, as were the Supremes, they were trapped in their hotel by mobs of teenage girls who had surrounded the building. They protested by staying high.

The Supremes, anxious to meet the top male vocal group of all time, performed their first show of the night at the Copa, and during the break before the second show they rushed to the Warwick to meet with the Beatles in their hotel room. You can feel their excitement as they hustled toward the Beatles' suite, imagining a glamorous, perhaps romantic meeting, and also perhaps sense their disappointment as they found the romantic British pop stars . . . playing with toys, giggling inexplicably, and behaving in an excessively silly manner. Flo was surprised to see that the four superstars "had little cars they would wind up and scoot across the floor. We had time to talk, but they were too busy playing with their cars. When I saw them doing that, I looked and said, 'They're kind of strange.'"

The meeting was marred by an awkward silence most of the time. One of the Beatles would ask the women a question, they would answer, and the silence would descend again. Then someone would tell a joke, and everyone would giggle nervously.

From the Beatles' point of view, as recounted in *The Beatles* by Bob Spitz, the Supremes looked like little porcelain figures outfitted in precious day dresses and little fur wraps. This surprised and disappointed the British singers, who had expected the Supremes to be rebels, as the Beatles imagined themselves to be. George Harrison later told Mary Wilson that the Beatles couldn't believe three black girls from Detroit could be so square.

The British thought that everything the Beatles did was outlandish. They desecrated the Union Jack by making fun of it! Their hair was too long! They sang like girls! Their accents were low class! What the Beatles perhaps hadn't realized was that the Supremes were going the other way entirely: they wanted to fit in with affluent whites and sell records to the respectable boys and girls whose mothers and fathers provided them with copious allowances. By seeking these goals, they were committing an implied and peaceful assault on segregation, but outside the South this was hardly a rebellion.

Since the Beatles were obviously eager to get back to other things, the Supremes left quickly, with the excuse that they had to rush back to the Copa for their second show.

But Flo rose above the incident and saw the bright side even when, in the view of others, a mini-fiasco had occurred. "They're some hell of writers," she said years later. "All the tunes they made I was crazy about. They have a lot of meaning to me."

Performing at major clubs required a special set of musicians who could easily work with, and keep up with, the Supremes. It also required many more costume changes than the women had been used to. In fact, the number of costume changes went from zero to twelve or more per show. The Supremes wore white gowns, multicolored sequined dresses, pink chiffon outfits, plain pink fitted dresses beaded across the bustline, green semiflair gowns with jackets that were beaded at the top, and of course their black outfits. They didn't stint on expenses. "Our personal dresses would cost maybe a hundred, two hundred; then we bought the perfume that cost so much an ounce. One year I spent $4,000 on clothes. That's not much, especially if you're a millionaire," Flo said sarcastically, reflecting what Gordy was telling her about her net worth.

The Supremes' financial situation worsened when the women started to let their popularity influence their spending. "We had charge accounts at Saks, Hudson's, and places like that," Florence said. "Whatever we charged, the bill didn't come to us; it went to Motown and was paid by Motown out of the account. We started buying stuff after we got that second million-seller ["Baby Love"]. We all got charge plates at Saks. We started buying nice clothes, $100 dresses [a high price in the 1960s]. Well, hell, we were millionaires—we had to dress like it. Plus we were playing at all the big, plush clubs. In other words we had to have a personal wardrobe that had to be sharp. We had to walk into the club sharp. Maybe we didn't have to, but we did. It was fantastic to be able to go out and buy everything we wanted and put it on and look like a million dollars."

The women often talked among themselves about the clubs at which they appeared. Flo couldn't shake the memory of an incident that occurred in Boston's Coconut Grove club. "I was in the dressing room, and the lamp fell off the table. The place started shaking. I didn't know they had earthquakes there. I never knew that. I said, 'God, why did the lamp fall off the table?' They said, 'Oh, that's an earth tremor.' I said, 'What!?' I was ready to get the hell out of there." (Some may be surprised to learn that Boston, like San Francisco, suffers from earthquakes. A quake in 1775 was strong enough to knock a statue off Boston's Faneuil Hall.)

Sometimes the Supremes were preceded by warm-up acts such as chorus lines or comedians, including Rodney Dangerfield and Flip Wilson. "We did a nightclub engagement in Cleveland, and Flip Wilson was just starting out; he was the comedian there," Flo said. "Flip had been trying for so many years, because we used to see him around different places we would go, and it seemed like Flip was just trying and trying. I'll never forget that he was starting out at those little bitty clubs and then, boom! He hit it big."

Logistically, the tours were arduous. "Whenever we did the Copacabana, that was for, like, two weeks," Florence said. "Then we would go to Boston and play at the club there for two weeks. We'd go back and forth at different times." The women would rush from the Clay House Inn in Bermuda to Blinstrubs in Boston to the Safari Room in San Jose to the Twin Coaches in Pittsburgh, back to Detroit, and then back out again.

The strain of constant work had been bearing down on them since their first hit. The Supremes' lives basically consisted of recording studio, nightclub performance, rehearsal, and bed—usually alone. Their social life was, and had to be, limited. They worked so constantly that they didn't have a chance to spend money on anything except their careers, and homes they rarely visited. (The women had all purchased homes, complete with mortgages, on the same street in Detroit.) A visitor to Diane's Detroit home concluded that the singer had never cooked on the stove nor even sat down in the kitchen, so rarely was she there.

Sometimes success made the Supremes paranoid and also stressed out their entourage. On one of their early tours, the Supremes' road manager whose job it was to collect the group's money at each engagement took in more than $100,000 in cash during the first five days of the tour. "We had so much Goddamn money I couldn't believe it," he said. He changed the money into thousand-dollar bills to reduce its bulk but still felt nervous carrying it around. Then he divided it for carrying purposes among the backup musicians, the three Supremes, and himself, but he still had nightmares. He eventually panicked, buying eight pistols, two each for himself and two each for three of the other men escorting the group. They all walked around warily with their thousand-dollar bills and their guns, but no one tried to rob them.

Although money was all around them, Flo had no idea how much the Supremes were earning or how much was being put aside for her. Neither did Mary and Diane. In their financial innocence, the Supremes were and still are joined by many other pop musicians whose inclinations, upbringing, and lifestyle, coupled with the traditions of the music business, can sometimes make them allergic to precisely the knowledge they need to protect their interests.

In spite of all the effort the Supremes were putting into their round-the-clock schedule, Flo said, "All the money we made would go back to Motown except for the allowance we were getting, $225 a week. We would get the gowns, but there was an account set up for the Supremes, and out of that account, whatever we bought, it was paid for by the Supremes account. . . . Motown never paid for anything. *We* paid for it. I didn't have a business mind. I didn't know that we should have seen the contracts. I should have known how much we were making for each engagement. The money should have been placed in our hands. The only thing they were supposed to take was their percentage, and the rest was supposedly to go to us."

The clubs they performed in may have varied, but the Supremes' act didn't, at least in its early days. "Every now and then maybe we'd take out a tune," Flo said. "If the first show would go overtime, then maybe we'd have to shorten the second show, and we'd just pull out a tune or something. And then sometimes we would add a new tune to the show. But basically the show stayed the same, stayed the same."

8

Room at the Top

They kept talking and talking and talking, look-
ing at us from the feet on up. I said, 'God, we
must be some kind of freaks.'"

—Florence Ballard, on an
experience in Japan

THE YEAR 1966 saw the Supremes in some surprising situations and locations as they toured the world.

Berry Gordy had become friends with Lord and Lady Londonderry, direct descendants of William the Conqueror. The name "Londonderry" has loomed large in British history ever since. The present Lord Londonderry is an intriguing and charming man. His second wife, Doreen Wells, was in the 1960s and early '70s the most acclaimed ballerina in Britain. That may explain why Lord Londonderry was interested in entertainers in the 1960s, and why Gordy sent the three very entertaining Supremes and their road manager to stay for more than a week at Lord and Lady Londonderry's stately home, also known as Wynyard Park.

Wynyard Park is not far from London, but in Flo's mind, they had been abandoned in the dark and dangerous English countryside. "It was very spooky," Flo said. "And so were Lord and Lady Londonderry. They looked like they were here and they weren't here. They were just the strangest-looking people to me. . . . I don't know where Berry Gordy came up with the idea for us to stay out there; I don't even know how he knew these people. Lord Londonderry showed me all around the estate, and I'm sorry I went, because he showed me their mausoleum. I saw it and said 'I'm getting the hell out of here, quick!' . . . I did not go into the mausoleum; I don't think any of us went in. The only place I'd seen anything like it was in the movies."

Florence was so shocked by the idea of entering a place of death that she didn't notice that at least one and possibly both of the other Supremes went inside the structure and admired it.

On high alert in the rural darkness, Flo soon realized that "the Londonderrys left us there. . . . And then I really became suspicious. The first night we ate in one of those big dining rooms with servants. I was looking out the window—it was pitch black out there, no lights—and I kept seeing something big moving. Turned out it was their Black Angus cattle.

"Then we all went to bed in adjoining rooms with all the doors all open between them. I got into bed, and my feet hit something. All three of us did the same thing. 'What the hell was that?' we all screamed and ran out and met up in the hall and then started laughing about it." The Londonderrys' servants had placed a hot water bottle in the bottom of each bed to warm their guests' feet.

"For a while it was just the three of us and our road manager, Donald Foster," Flo said. "Then Lord Londonderry came back and stayed a while. And I swear, every night we were all having us a drink. After a week we got kind of used to it. We figured out nothing was going to bother us. But I swear, when they said we were leaving, I looked up and said, 'Thank you, God.'"

In September 1966 the Supremes took off for Vietnam. "We were going to perform in Vietnam at first," said Flo, "but then they canceled out because the war was getting really bad there. They said they were bombing like mad. We were going to entertain the troops there and visit the hospitals. But we landed in Vietnam only for refueling. I'll never forget those airports, just pitch black, no lights whatsoever; at least I didn't see any, and they were telling us not to get off the plane at all, because they were putting fuel in the plane and then taking right back off.

"We took off and landed in Okinawa [Japan], and there we visited the hospitals and saw all the soldiers who had been wounded in Vietnam. . . . One guy was shot, and they didn't even have him bandaged; they'd just sewn him up, and the stitches were like a 'Z,' starting on his shoulder and all the way down. He had been shot by a machine gun. And this other guy, both his eyes were gone; a grenade had blown up in his face. He was touching us and saying, 'I'm just so happy that you all are here,' and he was holding on to us and said, 'I'm going back home now; I'm injured. They don't need me anymore here. But I'll be glad to get back to the States.'

"I looked at one guy, especially the guy that was shot with the machine gun, and my head started swirling. I got real dizzy, and I could hardly stand to look at all of them anymore, no legs, no arms. . . . I just got sick. . . . I'd heard about the war, how bad it was, and how the guys were being blown up and this and that, but to see it was—phew!—too much. We performed in the ward, singing along with the record, but I could hardly even sing along with the record. We had this little record player, and we were singing along with it and just doing dance steps. The ones that could see us could see us, and the ones that lost their eyes—they were just sitting and listening."

The three Detroiters went on to Manila, and then to Tokyo, where Flo encountered Asian curiosity. "We went shopping and were in this big store trying to buy this Japanese material to have some Japanese dresses made," Flo said. After about half an hour, "all of a sudden a large group of Japanese women" rushed over and surrounded them. "It scared the hell out of me because they had us in a circle. I didn't know whether they were going to attack, or what. I said, 'What's the problem?' and one girl who could speak English said they'd never seen black American women before. . . . They kept talking and talking and talking, looking at us from the feet on up. I said, 'God, we must be some kind of freaks.'"

In Tokyo, photographers took pictures of Flo, Mary, and Diane, who had since January started going by "Diana," dressed like geisha girls. Florence noted that the wigs they wore for these photos weighed twenty-five pounds each. Although the Supremes didn't perform in Hong Kong, they spent a day in that city, where Florence continued to react to the differences between Detroit and urban Asia. She noted that "these people were just living on top of each other, they would hang their clothes out, they lived in big buildings, they had clothes hanging out the window on lines. They'd be walking down the street smoking weed, marijuana, as if it was nothing. They had it in their pipes. They'd be walking down the street smoking it as if it was tobacco. I mean, you could smell it so thick." She segued into her own history, or lack thereof, with drugs.

"I don't smoke marijuana, although the majority of people I know do. I never tried any dope at all. I was always told when I was a child about dope. My mother really talked to me about marijuana. When I was a little girl, I never heard anything about heroin. As a matter of fact, I just learned how to pronounce 'heroin' about three years ago. I used to call it 'heron.' . . . I basically don't see anything wrong with smoking marijuana, but when it comes down to this cocaine, heroin, and stuff like that, then I got no use for you; you have to get away from me then."

The Supremes' earlier gig in Puerto Rico in January had been much more pleasant. "The people were enthusiastic about us. Plus, there were quite a few vacationing Americans there," Flo remembered. [Puerto Ricans also are Americans, but Flo's terms of reference are widely shared.] "They even had another lounge at the hotel where the Supremes were performing that featured Puerto Rican acts, so we would finish our show and then go over in the same hotel and watch the Puerto Rican show. Then we'd go over to old San Juan and do a little dancing. I danced with the Puerto Ricans I met there—nice, friendly gentlemen who never did anything out of the way. We'd just go down there after the show and dance and then go on upstairs and go to sleep, then get up and go to work."

It was in Puerto Rico that twenty-three-year-old Florence met a college student named Roger Pearson, "a white guy, very good looking," she said, with whom she had a relationship. "I swear he used to follow me everywhere," Flo said. "I'd look up, and there was Roger. He was a millionaire and very nice. I think his father owned Dreyfus Funds, or something like that. [Roger Pearson's father, Samuel Pearson, was in fact closely connected to the Dreyfus Fund and its founder, Jack Dreyfus. Samuel Pearson, Samuel Strasbourger, and Robert Tulcin were originally Dreyfus's partners in the 1960s.] He'd come out on the road, and we'd go out and have dinner and stuff like that together; then he'd leave and go back to college—that was that. He followed us anywhere, but only in the States. He popped up in Florida one time, and he popped up in Washington, D.C. I began to get used to him popping up.

"He would come to the room. He knew how to get through. Everybody knew him—Diane knew him, Mary knew him—he became just like a friend. . . . When we were playing in New York, he was in this steel gray Rolls-Royce. That was the first time I saw a Rolls-Royce. Berry Gordy didn't even have a Rolls-Royce then. He wanted to take me out that night in the Rolls-Royce after the performance, and I told him I was too tired. Very good-looking guy. Oh wow, I can imagine what he looks like now. Blue eyes . . . the sharpest physique in this world. But I don't know. The only thing I could be to him was a friend. I guess he just didn't appeal to me."

Today Roger Pearson is a successful attorney who has served as first selectman (mayor) of Greenwich, Connecticut, and ran unsuccessfully as the Democratic nominee for Congress in 1988 in Connecticut's Fourth Congressional District. Diana Ross also was a Greenwich resident, until 2006. Pearson said he met Diana Ross on a Greenwich street on one occasion, and she didn't recognize him. There's no doubt, however, that Flo would have recognized Pearson. "We were together for one and a half years. . . . We were pretty close. We were a couple," Pearson said, his definition of their relationship varying slightly from Flo's.

Pearson's recollection is that his first meeting with Flo took place while he and his brother Michael were vacationing in San Juan. To celebrate Roger's twentieth birthday, the two went looking for entertainment at the El San Juan Hotel, discovered that the Supremes were performing there, and bought tickets to the show. Pearson recalled, "They were a hit. They did a very slick show."

After the show he met Flo by chance in the hotel casino. "She looked at me, I looked at her, and I told her that I had enjoyed her music," he said. From then on they got together whenever they could. After the Supremes had finished a performance at the Yale Bowl, they all piled into his 1963 Pontiac Tempest and went bowling, but Flo had to cut the evening short because she split her pants, said Pearson.

On another occasion, after one of the group's shows at the Copa, their evening was dampened by the fact that there was a dead body with a sheet over it lying in the street outside. A New York City police officer had been arguing with a buddy when the friend became enraged and struck the officer on the head, killing him.

Pearson said that when he and Flo went out together in New York City in the 1960s, which they often did, he still felt slightly uneasy about other people's opinion of the daring step they were taking across the race barrier: "I never knew," he said, "if the stares were for her or for us or for both."

Pearson and Flo went out frequently during 1966 and the first half of 1967, including every night when the Supremes were performing at the Copa, Pearson said. Previously, he had served as a congressional intern and met then-congressman Gerald Ford in Washington, D.C. Later, after Pearson became friendly with the Supremes, he spotted the congressman in a Supremes audience when they were performing at a D.C. hotel and took the future president up to the Supremes' suite with him to visit with the women after the show.

In heady company for a college kid, Pearson spent his evenings in the Copa audience with celebrities such as Richard Burton, Sidney Poitier, Harry Belafonte, and Joe Louis and his nights dancing at the scorching hot Ginza nightclub in Manhattan with Flo, Diana, Mary, Martha Reeves, and Gordy.

From Flo's point of view, she said, "I liked guys I could have a lot of fun with. And I had a lot of fun with Roger because quite a few times we'd go out to dinner or we'd go to a discotheque and dance the monkey, the jerk, all that kind of stuff. We'd have a ball."

Pearson said the relationship ended because "you know how young people are. We drifted apart." He also noted, "Tommy Chapman came into her life about that time."

Thomas "Tommy" Chapman was "Berry's chauffeur, flunky, whatever you want to call it," said Flo. "Tommy would pack Gordy's stuff, his suit and clothes and this and that. He also worked with Mary.

"I was kind of a standoffish type," Flo said. "I wasn't that interested in too many guys. I never have been. One was always enough for me." She also discussed the love lives of her fellow Supremes: "Mary had a friend in Puerto Rico. . . . Very good-looking Puerto Rican. He was crazy about Mary; I mean *crazy*. He was real jealous. But she ended up marrying another Puerto Rican, Pedro Ferrer [Ferrer was from a Dominican family; his father was a banker in Puerto Rico]. . . . Diane dated Timmy Brown [of the Philadelphia Eagles]. . . . I don't think there was too much to it. That's the only person I can remember her dating, except for Berry Gordy."

By 1969 the gossip columns would call Gordy and Ross "constant companions," and the question most asked about them was why they didn't marry. Gordy said in 1970 that he and Ross "haven't chosen to be married for several reasons." Then he laughed and added that he had "tried to marry her a couple of times. But why should she marry me when she's got me already? She's free, rich, and talented. Get married for what?"

Shortly after Gordy issued this statement, Ross would become pregnant with Gordy's child, later named Rhonda. During the pregnancy she married Gordy's friend, a public relations executive named Robert Ellis Silberstein, who was aware of Rhonda's parentage. "The whole company is surprised and hurt by it," a Motown executive said of the marriage. The company may have been surprised and hurt, but Gordy's feelings at the time remain unclear. He and

Silberstein continued their friendship, often traveling together. Ross and Silberstein divorced in 1977, after having two daughters of their own. In October 1985, Ross married Norwegian businessman Arne Naess Jr. She saw a kindred spirit in Naess. He was divorced, had three children and, like Ross, had an ambition that wouldn't quit. "My ambitions are like a mountain without a summit," Naess once said. "When you have the top in sight, there's always another peak over the rise, further on and higher up." The couple had two sons but separated in 1999 and later divorced. Naess died in a mountain-climbing accident in Africa in 2004.

But Diana's romantic relationships were not uppermost in Flo's mind back in the mid- to late 1960s. She had her own deteriorating relationship with the Supremes to worry about.

9

Struggle Among the Stars

Flo was the one with the voice.

—Tony Turner, *All That Glittered: My Life with the Supremes*

THE SUPREMES HAD started as girlhood friends, worked their way to the top as hardworking young women, and gained international fame as talented, glamorous superstars. Along the way, their friendship had been sorely tested, and the struggle for each woman's position within the group had become increasingly bitter. Florence had been allowed to do the lead on "Buttered Popcorn" and on the Sam Cooke hit "Ain't That Good News." On *The Ed Sullivan Show*, Flo and Diana had performed "You Keep Me Hangin' On" almost as a duet, with Flo's strong voice filling out and underscoring every word sung by Diana. Flo's voice can also be heard in all its glory in the two other recorded Supremes songs in which she was featured as the lead, "Hey Baby" and "Heavenly Father." In Detroit, one critic had commented, "The group has two lead singers, and only one is being featured." Otis Williams of the Temptations wrote that Flo's voice "had a real depth of feeling and a strong churchy sound. When Flo opened her mouth to sing, you sat up in your chair."

But as the Supremes' star had risen, Florence had begun to feel her role diminish. In February 1963, when the group had been recording a country and western album on which Florence had been given the lead on one of the tunes, according to Flo, Diana broke off the recording, walked into the control room, and told the producers that she was the lead singer for all the songs. "Mary and I heard it through the earphones, and neither one of us could believe it," Flo said. "We had started out as children—that's what we were, fourteen or fifteen—and I felt that because of our relationship, because we were as close as I thought we were, the lead should have been spread around, as in 'You do this, and I'll do that.' But it wasn't. Diane wanted the complete lead, the complete control of the group."

And Diana kept getting what she wanted. Flo had originally been slated to sing the lead on "The House of the Rising Sun" on the Supremes album *A Bit of Liverpool,* but that was taken from her. She and Diana had shared the lead on the song "Manhattan," meant for *The Supremes Sing Rodgers & Hart,* but the song was cut from the album and not released until 1986, ten years after Flo's death. When Flo did the "Silent Night" lead for a Christmas album, the recorded track was mysteriously "messed up," in Flo's words, and not released for many years.

Flo's last remaining lead, in "People (Who Need People)," had been taken from her in one of several dramatic ways—depending on whom you believe—in the summer of 1965. (That the Supremes competed fiercely over who would do the lead on "People" and other tunes made popular by Barbra Streisand says much about the depth and doggedness of Gordy's crossover dream.)

The lead on "People" was tailor-made for Florence's soulful sound and not at all suited to Diane's voice, and at first the women were very democratic about it: Flo was assigned the lead at the beginning of the song, and Diana took the lead in the middle of the tune. Florence even thought the "People" lead should be spread around among all three singers. There was recent precedent for this—when the group had recorded a country album, each woman had sung a verse of the lead on one song, Willie Nelson's "It Makes No Difference Now." As Flo later said, "It's a heavy load to get up there and do two shows a night, with the lead on every song. But Diane wanted to be the lead singer on every song."

And Gordy agreed that she should be. According to Nelson George, author of *Where Did Our Love Go?*, Berry dismissed Flo's aspirations as a lead performer at a rehearsal at a Detroit nightclub, the Roostertail, in front of most of the Motown brass. Flo was allegedly only four bars into "People" when Gordy told her to stop. "Let Diana do the song," Gordy said. Flo flinched visibly and began crying, according to George.

According to Mary Wilson's account, however, the Copa was the site of a less dramatic scene. Wilson wrote that Harvey Fuqua, a Motown employee in charge of the company's Artist Development Department, merely "announced" that Flo would no longer perform "People." Many wondered about the announcement, since Flo had performed the tune on opening night at the Copa and, even though she had just recovered from the flu, sounded terrific. "A couple of nights later, however, Diane was singing it," Wilson wrote. According to Wilson, "We all suspected that Berry had taken the song from Flo, but Flo was thoroughly convinced of it, and she was crushed. How much more of the spotlight did Diane need? From that moment on, Flo regarded what was in fact the highest achievement of our career as a disaster. She was sad and moody, and I could see the three of us being torn apart."

Wilson wrote that Flo's response was to get defensive—"Understandably so. A talented singer and the founder of the group, Flo felt her professional existence was being threatened."

All Flo would say in 1975 was "They stopped me from singing the lead on 'People.' They said the show was too long or something."

With that, the battle for lead singer was effectively over, and Ross had won. While the undeniable commercial success of the combination of H-D-H songwriting and Diana's leads, coupled with her hard work and crossover appeal, may have made her the favored candidate for permanent lead Supreme, it was undoubtedly Berry Gordy's admiration of her that sealed the deal. His decision to back Diana totally over Flo also demonstrated how little Gordy cared about race and how much he cared about success and money. Diana epitomized style over substance and strove to look like Twiggy and Jackie Kennedy, two of the whitest women there ever were. Flo was just the opposite. She carried the essence of soul—a deep sadness—inside her and in her voice. Gordy believed correctly that whites preferred style to soul, and because whites were the major record buyers, he saw Ross as commercial success personified.

The "soul vs. success" controversy even extended to hair styles. During the Supremes' career thousands of fans wrote to them, urging them to wear their hair natural. They didn't; their white fans might not have understood. (After Flo left the Supremes, she wore her hair natural, as accurately portrayed by Jennifer Hudson in the *Dreamgirls* movie.) In March 1966 the women even allowed the name "Supremes" to be used as the name of a new white bread. Their photos appeared prominently on the crisp white wrappers.

Diana's push for vocal dominance succeeded, at a price. Apart from straining personal relationships, it also diminished the musical quality of the group. From then on, various Supremes producers urged Flo to stand far back from the microphone to prevent her distinctive, emotion-filled voice from overwhelming Ross's lead.

In the sense that teasing often reflects an underlying tension, a relative of Flo's had tried to slow Diana's grab for the glory. Winnie Brown, a niece of Flo's by marriage, traveled with the Supremes for a while as their hairdresser. Whenever the Supremes went on stage, Brown, a great joker and storyteller, would walk the Supremes to the wings of the stage, and then, when the Supremes were announced to the audience, maintain her grip on Diana's arm, literally holding her back while the other women walked out on stage. Brown mugged for the other women while holding on to Diana, making the meaning of her gesture all too clear. (Brown continued to protect Flo until the very end of Flo's life. After Flo's death in 1976, when her body was laid out for viewing, Brown did Flo's makeup and hair.)

Florence fought for the Supremes' musical purity as well as for her own role in the group. When the women were recruited in 1967 to record the title song for the movie *The Happening*, Gordy wanted to add three additional singers behind Flo and Mary to buttress Diana's lead. Flo objected, telling

Gordy, "Look Berry, we're getting paid for doing these tunes. I'm not going to work and have these other girls singing with me. . . . To me, they're not the group; they're just a whole bunch of other people. . . . We started off singing three together, and I think it should stay like that."

Gordy complied in this instance, but Flo's victory was short lived. Despite her objections, the voices of these singers, Jackie Hicks, Marlene Barrow, and Louvain Demps—called the Andantes—were added to several other Supremes tunes. Later, Ross's lead vocal was sometimes even recorded and mixed with *only* the Andantes' recorded voices so that records could be produced faster while all three Supremes were out performing live.

When the Andantes performed this service, it sometimes hurt the song. Otherwise decent songs such as "Forever Came Today," "The Composer," and "No Matter What Sign You Are," all backed by the Andantes, never rose higher than #28 on the charts.

Using substitutes for Flo and Mary was also a jolt for many Supremes fans. The three individual Supremes were featured on almost all Supremes album covers. On the cover of *The Supremes Sing More Hits*, they were distinguished not only by their individual photographs but also by each woman's autograph. In fact, Flo and Mary were quite possibly the only backup singers in rock 'n' roll history to have been identified by name in a verse of a hit in which the lead was sung by their major antagonist. Superfans of the Supremes might even interpret these lines in "Back in My Arms Again" as tailored to the pressures on each woman within the group. Diana sang, "How can Mary tell me what to do?" about the usually tongue-tied Wilson. And could "Flo, she don't know . . ." possibly be about Diana's plans to eliminate Flo from the group, even though the rest of the line is "the boy she loves is a Romeo"? Whatever the reasons for the references, they separated the group from the other female groups of the day. The Vandellas and the Marvelettes, for example, usually performed as a semi-nameless collective. The Supremes performed as three distinct women. The audience knew their names, who they were, and sometimes what they stood for.

The Andantes didn't profit much from their labor. "After Motown left Detroit [in 1972], they got different jobs," Flo said. "One moved to Atlanta. I saw one at the state fair, Jackie; she was working somewhere—I forget where. Just a common job." In show business terms, the women who had tried to imitate the original Supremes were never heard from again.

In any case, the feisty Florence Ballard continued to fight against her diminishing role in the group she had founded by speaking up on behalf of what she perceived to be group interests. "In between [nightclub acts], if we came home," Flo said, "we'd be doing recording. We never really had that much of a vacation, and I believe that sometimes we were overworked, 'cause we worked practically the whole year without a break. And if we did come to Detroit, we were working because we were still recording, which is a job too. I objected—me—and Berry Gordy said I was the one who would always sit down, always think. I'm always thinking. I'm the type of person if I can't think, then something is wrong. So we were in New York one time, and he said, 'You girls are off for ten days, but I don't think I'll let you have a vacation, because Florence talks too much.'"

Flo's underlying aim had been to reassert some of her leadership of the group, but Gordy's reaction did not exactly buttress her position or even make her popular with her sidekicks.

Flo also fought back in other, counterproductive ways. Right or wrong, she believed that her founding and early domination of the group, along with her talent, should have made her the Supremes' permanent leader and that she should have the enduring right to sing the lead on at least some songs. When leadership was denied her, she sometimes became sullen and angry. Generally happy, playful, and funny, she could also display a quick temper and sometimes responded to what she interpreted as insults, or attempts to limit her freedom, by challenging the offender verbally or even physically. It has been alleged that on one occasion she threw a drink in Gordy's face, which, if true, certainly would have made her situation worse.

Soon Flo discovered another outlet for her anger and frustration: comedy. "I said, 'I can't sing "People" anymore; I'll start doing some comedy.' It just dropped out of the sky. Growing up, I used to jump around and kid around and this and that, but I never knew I had comedy potential."

Following a Motown script of onstage banter, Diana had started referring to Flo, on stage behind her, as "the fat one." One night Flo retorted—deep-voiced, sotto voce, and unscripted—"Honey, fat is where it's at." Laughter engulfed the crowd, and Sammy Davis Jr., who was in the audience, jumped straight into the air out of his seat and began applauding wildly, as did Harry Belafonte. Flo had neither planned this event nor anticipated the audience reaction, and her boldness frightened her.

"I was shocked. I was looking around and saying to myself, 'What did I do? Where did I get the nerve to interrupt the act?' I didn't even know I was that funny. It just came out of my mouth, out of nowhere. I was just ad-libbing on stage. Berry Gordy came backstage after the performance and told me, 'You stole the show.' And I said to myself, 'Uh-oh, stole the show,' and worried even more."

After her worry subsided, however, she began planning her guerrilla attacks in advance. "One song had a line, 'Gold won't bring you happiness.' And I'd say, 'Wait a minute honey. Give me some of that gold, and I'll do my own shopping.'" Another version of this dialogue emerged when Diana would sing, "You may be rich; you may possess the world and all its gold, but gold won't bring you happiness when you're growing old," and Flo would respond, "Now wait a minute, honey; I'm not so sure about that."

Flo was stretching when she called this comedy. It may have struck the audience as wildly amusing, but in reality Flo was clearly protesting being shunted to the sidelines by calling attention to herself.

"After a while," Flo recalled, "I knew exactly what to say and how to say it. I would wait until the audience had stopped applauding and then deliver another line. And that started them off again." Her fans compared her to Pearl

Bailey, "and I used to watch Pearl Bailey as a child, but I never tried to imitate her. It was just that people thought I had that flat type of heavy voice, and I just came across as if I were imitating her, but actually I wasn't. I was never imitating anybody except myself, if you can believe it, just myself.

"I'm a strong believer in God, and I don't know where the words came from or what happened, but it just happened, and that was it. Whenever I saw a spot where I could get it in, then I would get it in. . . . Berry Gordy liked what I was doing, because he would come backstage to try to perfect my comedy, 'Say it this way; say it that way.' But I had to say it my way. . . . Saying it my way kept it coming across."

At the Coconut Grove, where the group performed for a doctor's convention, "Diane would say, 'At the end is Florence Ballard. She's the quiet one.' I would be way back from the mike. And I would say, 'That's what *you* think.'"

The audience laughed loudly.

10

The Corner of Hollywood and Woodward

Berry wanted to merge into a big movie company, but probably those big white movie companies said, 'Uh-uh, Brother, no.'

—Florence Ballard

It was Flo in whom Gordy first saw Hollywood potential.

Gordy's filmmaking overture to Florence was preceded by a semiromantic overture. He had warmed up to the statuesque Supreme in London on the Supremes' triumphant tour there. "Gordy wanted to take me out that night, so he took me to a club in Soho," Flo said. "This girl was dancing with a snake or something—I don't know, something weird, a weird bit—and he used to always tell me I needed to grow up. So I guess maybe he took me there so I could grow up, could see what was going on. The act was ridiculous! The snake was all around her arm. She was doing some weird things with the snake. I told him I was ready to go. And he said, 'You should see things like that. That's a part of growing up.' But we left."

At times, Gordy seemed concerned with Flo's sexual education. "He even told me one time it was circulating through the company that I was a virgin . . . that he felt I should know more about life." In 1975, Flo was still able to joke about this incident. When she told this story, the mother of three added "and to this day I'd like to find out what he meant!" and then giggled.

Perhaps Gordy truly believed Flo should expose herself to adult entertainment, but he may also have had hopeful thoughts about what her reaction might be. "I'm sure Berry liked me," Flo said. "I don't mean liked me maybe sexually or intimately or anything like that. But I'm sure he felt something for me. I'll never forget one time he bought me a suede suit for no reason. I still have the suit. And he didn't buy the other girls one. It was weird. . . . He told me, 'I saw this suit, and I thought it would look good on you.'"

Motown insiders remember seeing Gordy and his father, "Pops" Gordy, standing together in company headquarters when Florence walked by. The old man would invariably whistle appreciatively in her direction.

Flo recalled that a short while after Gordy's attentions to her, he put her in a film. "We were over in Asia, and he had these guys with these cameras, and he actually had me doing a movie running up and down the street, you know, just playing around. Everybody saw the movie but me. And I asked them what happened to the movie, and they said it wasn't any good. But everybody else had seen it; I couldn't understand how come I couldn't see it. . . . That's when Berry first had that thing in his mind about movies."

Later, in Paris, "Berry Gordy had this big film thing going," Flo continued. "So he would hide these guys with the movie cameras, and he had us running up and down the streets in Paris, and the police got upset because we were messing up the traffic there. The police told us to cut it out, but Berry told Diane to keep on going. Berry Gordy's a powerful black guy, you know. The policeman had a paper in his hand; I think he popped Diane with it. She got mad about it, I think, but I don't think she was brave enough to pop him back. Anyway, they were right; we had no business in the street because we could have got hit."

Although Gordy never really dropped his enthusiasm for movies in general, for some reason he soon changed his mind about Florence's participation in them. The group was doing a show at the Fairmont Hotel in San

Francisco, recalled Flo, "and Berry was sitting in the audience between two big movie producers. He came backstage—it wasn't even on my mind to go into movies—and he says, 'Those were two movie producers I was sitting out there with, and they picked you, Florence, but I told them that you were just a deadpan and that Diane works the hardest, so she should be the one to do the movies.'

"I was startled, I was shocked. . . . I was hurt, very hurt," Flo said, "because I had never thought of doing a movie, but for him to come back there and say that . . . if it had been me, I never would have said anything."

Flo was still bitter about these movie-related incidents years later. "Some people say the Mafia ran Berry out of Detroit, but I don't believe it. I believe he went to Los Angeles to try and be a big movie guy. Berry wanted to merge into a big movie company, but probably those big white movie companies said, 'Uh-uh, Brother, no.' If you notice, the only people doing movies with Diane is Berry Gordy. No one else is offering her a part that I know of."

Flo was correct. Gordy ended up producing, in descending order of artistic excellence and profitability, *Lady Sings the Blues*, *Mahogany*, and *The Wiz*, all starring Diana Ross. In *Lady*, Diana played singer Billie Holiday, which featured Ross's singing more than her acting talents. In *Mahogany*, in which she played a fashion designer, her acting talents were not impressive. In *The Wiz*, Gordy shoehorned the thirty-three-year-old Ross into the role of Dorothy, a part made for a twelve-year-old that Judy Garland barely qualified for at age sixteen. As a result, *The Wiz*, while definitely a spectacle, was anything but an emotional grabber. Although Diana later appeared in a couple of made-for-TV productions, she never received a part in another Hollywood movie.

Not that Gordy didn't consider other movie roles for Diana. Ross and Billy Dee Williams, her costar in *Mahogany*, were going to star in a movie to be called *Sesame Linday*, about a bail bondswoman and a Berkeley economics professor. Gordy also considered starring both of them in an untitled movie to be based in New Orleans, and he weighed starring Ross in a movie to be called *Tough Customers,* in which she would have played a Harlem numbers queen who fell in love with a white, Jewish gangster. This film idea may have been inspired by her marriage to Silberstein in 1971, even though Silberstein was no gangster.

As it turned out, however, the failure of *The Wiz* would not only end Ross's movie career; it would also eliminate Motown as a major movie producer. Critics have argued that Florence, more statuesque, more capable of a range of emotions than Ross, and gifted with comic potential, could well have done better than Diana. We'll never know.

The Supremes: Diane Ross, Florence Ballard, and Mary Wilson. *Roger Williams*

Florence Ballard, Queen of Motown.

The Andrew Skurow Collection

The iconic Supremes.

Author's collection

The Supremes were the Primettes before they became the Supremes. Their male equivalents were the Primes—later named the Temptations. Seated is Otis Williams, with whom Flo had a brief relationship. *Al Abrams*

The Supremes performing at the Copacabana in 1965. *Frances Baugh*

The Supremes celebrating their #1 status. *Jim Lopes*

The Supremes autographing albums for their fans. *Al Abrams*

Flo and Pearson outside the Rickshaw Inn,
Cherry Hill, New Jersey. *Roger J. Pearson*

Flo and boyfriend Roger Pearson, 1967.

Roger J. Pearson

*The Andrew
Skurow
Collection*

The Supremes try to act natural despite their seasonal headgear. *Jim Lopes*

Flo looking angry, Diana looking complacent, and Lord Londonderry looking sleepily puzzled during the Supremes' stay at his stately home outside London. *Alastair Londonderry*

Flo posing for an ABC promotional still during her post-Supremes campaign for solo stardom. *The Andrew Skurow Collection*

Diane, Flo, and Mary arriving at Lord Londonderry's home. *Alastair Londonderry*

Flo with husband Tommy Chapman in 1968, outside Saks Fifth Avenue in Detroit.

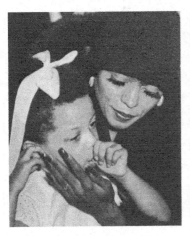

Diana Ross and Flo's daughter Lisa Ballard Chapman at Florence's funeral. *Detroit Free Press.*

Florence Ballard's death certificate. Cause of death: coronary artery thrombosis.

City of Detroit

Flo's daughters with Mary Wilson in 1988. Left to right: Nicole Ballard Chapman, Mary Wilson, Michelle Ballard Chapman, and Lisa Ballard Chapman.

Steve Holsey, The Michigan Chronicle

11
Trouble at the Top

I knew a Diane that was a monster.

—Florence Ballard, 1975

AS GORDY'S ATTRACTION to and admiration of Flo waned, his criticism of her began. "He would say, 'Flo, you don't know how to be a star,'" she said, "and maybe I didn't, because as far as I was concerned, I was a person, and I had to be a person. I couldn't be anything else. It's frightening to go all the way to the top, and somebody says to you that you have to be a star, that you can't mingle with certain people. People, to me, has always meant people, and I've always felt that if I don't have people, then I don't have anything; and I still feel that way. I was supposed to carry myself like a star. I knew I was a big entertainer, I knew I was rich, I knew I was making lots of money; I knew this. I had beautiful clothes, diamonds, everything at my feet; but to me a star is something in the sky, and to me I was a human being.

"Berry was talking about mingling. I would always talk to people instead of rushing and jumping into the car, fans and this and that. I would always stop and talk, and I just couldn't break the habit. Mary was very good at it, but me, I would linger."

"Flo was always her own person," her friend Pat Cosby said. "She realized we have to be dictated to in life. There has to be a leader. But she knew who she was. . . . Flo never got lost in the fame, as far as her personality and as far as being herself. You have to be a strong individual not to get yourself lost in that."

Flo was not only strong but also ahead of her times. She tried writing some songs for the Supremes. "Yeah, I tried; I sure did try, and Berry Gordy said, 'Hm, that ain't nothing.' The other girls thought it was pretty good. But I don't know. For some reason, me and Berry didn't click."

A few years later, the majority of the top-selling hits would be written by the artists performing them. The singer-songwriter became an icon. Marvin Gaye and Stevie Wonder began trying to convince Motown to allow them to write and produce their own songs. Motown refused, leading to major strains between the company and its creative artists.

Otis Williams wrote that when the Temptations formally asked Gordy for the publishing rights to songs they wrote, Gordy replied, "'What are you going to do with publishing? Who's going to administer it?' [Music publishing involves giving others permission to record or use your songs, and collecting for that usage. It can be a very lucrative business and certainly has been for Motown.] He continued running down all the details," and as he did so became angrier and angrier. "We looked at one another as if to say, 'Whew! We really touched a nerve with this!' We'd never seen him so angry."

In spite of, or perhaps because of, Flo's attempts to relate to the fans and to increase her contributions to the Supremes, Diana's ambitions grew, and, according to Flo, her treatment of her girlhood friends became atrocious.

Pointing out that "Diane always tried to hog the show" and "Diane is very ambitious," Florence recalled, "We had a routine when performing 'Stop! In the Name of Love' where at the end of the tune we'd throw both arms up in the air. Well, people used to ask me, 'Why did Diane always get in front of Mary, right in front of her when she threw her arms up?' blocking Mary completely from view.

"And it got to the point, I'll never forget, one time, while we were performing in Boston, Diane's mike went out, so without any warning at all she walked over and snatched Mary's microphone out of her hand. Mary snatched it back. Here they are snatching this microphone back and forth, and I'm standing there still singing and looking at them. You know what should have happened was, Diane should have said, 'My mike is out,' and just started singing on the same mike with Mary. It could have been done like that. But she walked over and actually snatched that mike. It's funny, but it was ridiculous too."

Flo, by contrast, came to Diana's aid during another Boston performance in April 1966. "We were singing the tune 'I Hear a Symphony,' and everything was fine with me and Mary; we were singing the background, just singing back, and all of a sudden Diane began to back up away from the microphone, real slow. She said, 'I feel so little. Everything looks so tiny. I feel like I'm shrinking.' I said, 'What!?' She was holding her head." Mary and Flo kept on doing the background until the song was completed, "and then we went offstage too, and our road manager at the time, George McArthur, picked Diane up and carried her into her dressing room.

"That's when I called Berry Gordy and told him that Diane couldn't perform, she was ill. I had her head in my lap, and I was trying to massage her head, and she was just moving her head from side to side and crying, and she said the pain in her head was so . . .

"Berry Gordy flew in, and we went back to Detroit; and she went into Ford Hospital in Detroit.

"The nurses, when I went in [in 1968] to have my twins, they were telling me how nasty she was when she was in the hospital." Florence defended her longtime persecutor. "I said, 'Well, she was ill, though,' and the nurses said, 'We were trying to be nice to her; we knew she was ill.' They said she slammed the door in their face and carried on. To this day, this day, they haven't forgotten her; they have never forgotten her for that."

According to Flo, Diana did not reciprocate when their situations were reversed. Ironically, the group was performing in Boston to raise money to fight disease, when a disease dropped Flo. "I came down with pneumonia. We had been overseas, and the doctor said what happened was I had caught the flu over in Europe and was carrying it in my system, and all of a sudden it just hit me.

"I couldn't perform because my throat was so sore and I was so weak. . . . And Diane looked at me and said, 'You know you're not sick.' The way she looked at me was very vicious. She said, 'You're not sick. There's nothing wrong with you.' Later on, Diane said to me in the car, 'I don't think you should be in the car with us, because whatever you've got is probably catching.' She was very nasty. That really hurt, sick as I was. And I said she's got to be the nastiest ass in the world. I went back to Detroit, and I could barely walk or anything. My temperature kept going up, and the doctor told me I couldn't perform. . . . But she insisted that I just wasn't sick. I don't know what was wrong with her."

After the group returned from Boston and was rehearsing in Detroit, Florence recovered enough to go over and join the rehearsal and was greeted by Diana. "'What are you doing here?' she said, and I just looked at her, and finally said, 'What do you think I'm doing here?' and she said, 'Well, nobody told you to come here.' Oh, she was very nasty; she was very, very nasty. I told her nobody had to tell me to come, but I was told to come because there was a rehearsal going on; and they knew, Cholly Atkins and all of them, they knew I had been ill, but they told me to come anyway so I could just sit and watch and learn that way."

Shortly afterward, Motown showed how much it cared about Flo when its employees were taping a television performance on Belle Isle, an island in the Detroit River. "Berry talked to my doctor, Dr. Carlson, and asked if it would be OK if I did the TV show. Dr. Carlson said 'Actually, I don't think that she should, but if she's out there for just one hour, then it's OK.' I was out there from 9:00 in the morning until 6:00 that evening, and from that I had a relapse.

"They knew I was only supposed to be out there an hour, and when I was out there, I began to get sick. I told them, 'Hey, I have to go because I'm not feeling well,' and they kept saying, 'Well, we'll be taping you all pretty soon now, pretty soon now.' Pretty soon never came, and Berry just didn't give a damn. All he could think about was 'Look, there's money to be made. I don't give a damn if you're sick or what.' That's when I began to . . . look at him in a different way altogether, and as far as I was concerned, he was just a sadist, a selfish, vicious man. Sure he's a genius, he made a lot of money . . . but the truth is the truth.

"All my joints were inflamed, and I went from a size 12 to a size 7 in about two weeks. I just couldn't move. If I tried to move my arms, it was just so painful I just couldn't do it. . . . The doctor kept giving me vitamin B-12 shots, which finally worked. . . . But Diane didn't even come over to see me when I was sick. I don't know what made Diane like that, because when we were growing up, she always wanted to be the best at everything, and there's nothing wrong with that; but when you try to step on other people, I don't know, somewhere along the line you're going to get stepped on someday. Of course," Flo said in 1975, "she's doing real well now, moviewise and this and that, but I guess that's what Berry Gordy wanted: Diane to be a star."

Occasionally, Diana broke the pattern by supporting Flo against Gordy. "We were going to take some pictures in front of one of the [Detroit] high schools, and Diane and Mary and I were trying to decide which high school to use, whether Cass, Northeastern, or Northwestern, and I said it really didn't make me any difference. So Berry Gordy said something I'll never forget; he said, 'I can see why it doesn't make any difference to you, Flo, since you never finished high school.' So Diane looked at him and said, 'Well, you didn't finish high school either, Berry.' It was the one time she stood up for me."

In general, though, Diana attacked Flo, and Flo responded. "I didn't take no stuff off Diana," Flo said. "If she said something to me, I'll say it back to her."

Pat Cosby noted that "Florence was always very honest. She didn't hold back her thoughts." No one who knew Flo would disagree, but that doesn't mean some people didn't advise her to act differently.

"Mary would always tell me, 'Whatever she says to you, don't say anything back to her, because you know what they want you to do—they want you to keep arguing back and forth so they can get you out of the group.'

"This was the first I'd heard of that. I told Mary that if Diane said something mean to me, I'm going to say it back to her. So she would say a few words to me I didn't like, and I would tell her to go to hell and a lot of other things.

"I couldn't understand exactly what was going on. The three of us didn't do things together anymore. The only time we'd see each other would be in a dressing room or onstage. And our rooms were all on different floors and miles apart."

Mary had her emotions much more locked down. Flo said, "I'll never forget when Diana walked into the dressing room in Las Vegas and found these [false] eyelashes on the floor. She picked them up and said, 'Humph! These couldn't be nobody's eyelashes but Mary's because they're very dirty.' Mary didn't say anything back to her. If it had been me, I would have let her have it, but Mary just held it in. And I didn't think it was fair that I should hold it in, or Mary should hold it in, because Diane wasn't no queen—not to me—and she still isn't."

Meanwhile, rumors were circulating feverishly that Diana would be leaving the group to perform on her own. Mary, in a tribute to Florence's voice and performing ability, claimed, "I still retained the smallest hope that when and if Diane left, Flo would be made the lead singer."

Diana remained a queen to Gordy, however, and Flo sank further and further in his estimation. "It seemed like I was always under pressure from Berry," she said. "I remember we were in Canada getting ready to catch a flight in Vancouver in 1966, and just out of the clear blue he walks up to me and says, 'You know, you told me you wouldn't try to stand in Diane's way if she wanted to be a single artist.' And I told him, 'That's right, I wouldn't stand in the way if she wanted to be a single artist, but by the same token, I didn't say I would leave the group either.' So it went on and on and on."

Flo's increasingly precarious position in the Supremes became vividly clear to her in May 1967, when, she recalled, "We got to the Copacabana, and Cindy Birdsong [a singer who had substituted for Flo on one occasion] was there. They had been grooming her with tapes for a whole year, and I didn't even have any knowledge of it. They had a whole tape of the show we were doing, the nightclub act, so she was learning the tunes and everything with the tape. Having Cindy at the Copa caused me to feel more pressure because it was as if they were saying, 'We're getting ready to put you out now.' I was thinking, 'I may be out, I may be in,' that sort of thing, but I was trying to keep calm about it and not worry about it, about what they were saying. But I was wondering, 'Am I in or Am I out?'

"I lay down in the dressing room in Las Vegas, and I looked up at the ceiling, and I said, 'God, what's happening? . . .' I was scared, unhappy; it was a whole bunch of mixed-up feelings."

When the limousine pulled up in front of the hotel to take the women to the Copacabana, "Instead of me getting in the limousine, Cindy Birdsong was asked to get in the limousine," Flo remembered.

"So I rode to the Copa in a Lincoln that Tommy [Chapman] was driving. Cindy was there mainly to study me, to study my performance. We finished the engagement at the Copa, and I don't know which way Cindy Birdsong went after that. We went on and worked the Coconut Grove, and then we went to Las Vegas. That was at the Flamingo Hotel in July 1967: that's when I made my last performance with the Supremes."

As if parading Flo's replacement in front of her and giving that replacement Flo's seat in the limousine didn't send Flo the message Gordy wanted her to hear, he had also been thickening the steady stream of criticism he directed at her. "Berry . . . knew how to get to me, because he always said he wanted to control me, and if he couldn't control me, he didn't want me around," Flo said. "So I guess by being controlled, I was supposed to be a puppet on a string, and he was supposed to pull my string, and then I'd dance to his tune. Well, I'm not that type of person, and I don't dance to anyone's tune, unless I want to.

"Berry's a weird dude, very weird. . . . Funny thing about Berry, I'll never forget, he had a blue suit, and this other guy who worked for Berry had one just like it. He told the guy he couldn't wear the suit, and the guy actually didn't wear the suit anymore. And I say all these guys running around letting Berry put the stuff on them, I mean, telling them what to do, like you're my slaves—you do what I do, you do not dress like I dress, you do not look like I look. . . . I don't have any use for people like that. Because as far as I'm concerned, they're not people. I don't know what you call them, but they're not people."

The contrast could not be clearer between Flo and Mary Wilson, who did everything she was told until the original Supremes broke up, and Diana Ross, who almost always made sure well in advance that Gordy would give her only the directions she wanted to hear.

The contrast between Flo and Diana was unmistakable in another way. As Flo put it, "Boy, was I stacked." Gordy, not really into this sort of statuesque beauty, considered Florence fat. "That was something Berry Gordy always used to say," Florence said. "He used to have a line whereas he'd tell me, 'Florence, for you to be a fat girl, you don't sweat that much,' whatever that meant. Sometimes he'd just out and tell me, 'Florence, you're too fat.' Well, I was a size 12, and I guess next to Diane maybe I was fat, but as far as I was concerned, I was pretty damned stacked. I got pictures to prove that; I just had a nice body. You know, size 12, five foot seven, that's a perfect size. I'm a 14 now [in 1975], and that's not a bad size, not for my height and my bone structure. I wasn't meant to be skinny.

"Some places we played, especially in Manila, they didn't even pay anyone any attention but me. The guys' reaction in the audience were something else. I accumulated so many, call it, fans, but I would say friends also, and they were mostly male, and they were very nice, and I enjoyed it. One little guy ran up to the stage and he said, 'Oh, Florence, I just love you, baby.' It was fantastic. So I must have had something on the ball that wasn't fat. I'll never forget Berry Gordy saying, 'Wow, these guys are going crazy over you here, you're really on the ball.' He said it in a very nice way, but they were after me."

The issue of Flo's weight and the varying reaction it engendered had already appeared in joke form in the Supremes' stage patter. Under the thin veneer of humor, the women played out their very real personal conflicts in front of audiences that dimly understood what was happening.

Soon, however, Gordy began teasing Flo about something other than her weight. "He'd say, 'Florence, you drink too much,'" according to Flo. Her initial reaction was "In other words, I guess I was supposed to say I was an alcoholic, from drinking two or three beers [a day]."

Flo acknowledged that the Supremes drank casually in nightclubs, even when they were performing. "That was not unusual," she said. "Mary, Diane, all of us had drinks before we went onstage, or any time we felt like it." But she was also aware that she was sinking into depression as it became increasingly obvious to her that an effort was under way to eject her from the group, noting, "To be depressed and to drink with depression can cause a whole bunch of turmoil, especially when you are actually angered, as I was toward Berry, and I just began to lose all respect for him, because I'll never forget how he used to sit in the audience with his sunglasses on, and he had his hair in a process, you know, straightened, and he just didn't look like what he was supposed to be. And I just didn't have any respect for him at all, and I still don't."

Flo's anger at Gordy and his effort to push her out of the group she had founded caused her to push her drinking, and her aggressive behavior, to a new level. Mary Wilson wrote, "Diane and I could drink without suffering any ill effects, but Flo's tolerance for alcohol was almost nil. After just one beer, she would be unsteady; any more than that, and she was clearly intoxicated."

On Flo's last night performing as a Supreme, she recalled, "At this particular incident at the Flamingo in Las Vegas, I had had me a few drinks. . . .

And they kept calling me fat so much until I went on stage and I poked my stomach out as far as I could." Alcohol had undoubtedly clouded Flo's judgment, and this time, it would seem, she'd had gone too far, giving Gordy the excuse he'd been looking for to cut her out of the group.

Gordy "called me up the next morning and he said, 'You're fired.' And I said, 'I'm what?' And he said, 'You're fired.' I said, 'I'm not.' And he said, 'Well, you're not going onstage tonight.' I said, 'Yes, I am; who's going to stop me?' He said, 'I will. I'll have you thrown off if you go on.' So it went on and on and on. I told him, 'I'm going onstage, and that's the end of that,' and hung up. And then his sister, Gwen Gordy, called and said, 'I guess you know that my brother can't make you leave the group, because you have a contract.' So it went on and on and on until finally I said to myself, 'Oh, well, what the hell, I'll be miserable as hell out here anyways as long as he's around, so I just might as well leave.' So I left. They had Cindy already there. I don't know how long she had been there, but they had had her there, and I flew on back to Detroit."

With that, what *Variety* had referred to as the "superb distinctive blend" of Ballard, Wilson, and Ross was over. Florence Ballard was only twenty-four years old.

Although to some extent Flo may have brought on the expulsion herself, the effect on her was crushing. Being kicked out of the Supremes "stole her spirit and stole her energy," Roger Pearson said. "Flo felt something important had been stolen from her." Millions of Supremes fans believe there was something magical about the Supremes that the breakup ended forever. "Their three personalities formed a fourth, the Supremes," Pearson said. Florence's later decline, he insisted, was due to her inability to handle the impact of this betrayal, not any inability to handle fame.

Flo's expulsion from the Supremes in the summer of 1967 was immediately followed by the renaming of the group "Diana Ross and the Supremes." The meaning and the symbolism were obvious. With her major rival for lead singer finally out of the way, Diana Ross could take over the Supremes in name and in actuality. But the renaming meant more than that. Putting Diana's name out front was an invitation to the public to view her as separate from the other Supremes. It was the first step toward Gordy's ultimate goal of moving Ross out of the group and into solo stardom.

Record producer Weldon McDougal III, a Motown employee at the time, insists that the only reason Birdsong was chosen to replace Flo "was because she could wear the same size gowns Flo wore. They didn't want to make the gowns all over again." McDougal is exaggerating—this was *one* of the reasons Birdsong was selected—but it puts to rest the oft-repeated argument that Flo was fired because of her weight. Her occasional sullenness, her occasional protests, her occasional drinking, Gordy's attitude toward her, and his desire to make Diana a solo superstar were the real causes.

And, as Flo noted, Motown had her replacement waiting in the wings. Born Cynthia Ann Birdsong in 1939, Cindy Birdsong was, like Flo, a founding member of her group. Together with her friend Patricia Louise Holt, Birdsong created a four-member girl group called the Ordettes in 1958. When two of the original Ordettes left the group in 1959, Holt and Birdsong brought in singers Nona Hendryx and Sarah Dash. The young women sang locally for two years until they auditioned for Blue Note Records. After they signed with Blue Note, they changed their name and spent another two years singing before they started producing hits. Does any of this sound familiar?

Alfred Lion, president of Blue Note, had been about to reject the group because he didn't think Holt, the lead singer, was pretty enough to carry the group to stardom. He changed his mind, though, when Holt opened her mouth and the voice of a torch diva came out, a voice very much like Flo's. Disliking the name "Ordettes," he signed them to his label on the condition that the name of the group be changed to the "Bluebelles." He also decided to conquer what he perceived as Holt's appearance problem by changing her name too. She became Patti LaBelle—Patti the Beautiful. Lion had to alter his course slightly when he started hearing unpleasant words from the manager of a group that was already named "Bluebelles," so he changed the name of the group to "Patti LaBelle & the Bluebelles."

Patti LaBelle & the Bluebelles remained more tied to their African American roots than did the Supremes and scored hits with "I Sold My Heart to the Junkman" and "Down the Aisle." The group then moved to Atlantic Records in 1966 and anticipated Diana Ross's role in *The Wiz* by recording a hit version of "Somewhere over the Rainbow," the Judy Garland song from *The Wiz* predecessor *The Wizard of Oz.* Patti LaBelle's resemblance to Flo became much more up close and personal when she became engaged to Otis Williams, Flo's former boyfriend. Their conflicting tour schedules caused Williams and LaBelle to eventually break their engagement, just as similar factors had broken up Williams and Flo. LaBelle suffered another blow when Birdsong left the group to take Flo's place in the Supremes, just as Wilson and Birdsong of the new Supremes were hurt shortly thereafter when Diana Ross left for solo stardom. The coincidences just kept on coming until Patti LaBelle left the group to begin her long-running, successful solo career.

Motown's official announcement said that Flo had left the group owing to exhaustion and a desire to settle down. A story in the *Detroit Free Press* in August 1967 said that Florence was leaving the group for only a month. A *Detroit News* story based on an interview with Ross and Wilson indicated that the issue had been one of time off for the women and that the two remaining Supremes had told Motown that they needed one week off every six weeks, or two weeks off every three months. A story in yet a third publication said that Flo was leaving the group to go into the antiques business. This cloud of deception would not be dispersed until Flo sued Motown three years later.

12

After the Fall

*You're not supposed to ever say that you were a
Supreme, or had anything to do with the Supremes
whatsoever. . . . In other words, you're nothing.*

—Florence Ballard

FLORENCE left Las Vegas, returned to Detroit, and met with Motown vice president Michael Roshkind on July 27, 1967, a week after she had been fired as a Supreme. Roshkind offered her a release to sign. "I read a little bit of it that said you're not supposed to ever say that you were a Supreme, or had anything to do with the Supremes whatsoever. You can never call yourself an ex-Supreme."

For Flo, being stripped of her identity as a Supreme was of totemic importance. "It has been disputed and disputed and disputed who thought up the name 'Supremes,'" Flo said. "But I chose the name 'Supremes' . . . and Berry Gordy took the name from me. And he tried to take the 'Jackson Five' name too. How can you take the 'Jackson Five' name when that's their last name, Jackson?" Later, Mary Wilson would also become determined to retain her right to the name. In fact, Wilson sued Gordy and Motown for that right in 1977. Diana would appear to be less reverent toward the name "The Supremes," first by putting her own name in front of it and then by leaving it behind entirely.

Now Motown's agreement stipulated that Flo, who had founded the Supremes and chosen its name, would not be allowed to use that name to help her own career. The agreement also said she would not receive any future royalties from Motown, even on hits she already had recorded.

"In other words, you're nothing," Florence said, "and Michael Roshkind's saying if you don't sign the paper, Berry Gordy won't have anything else to do with you. I told Michael Roshkind I really didn't give a damn whether Berry Gordy had anything to do with me or not. . . . Then I started crying and I signed the paper. I didn't even finish reading it.

"Anyway, it said all you are worth is $15,000. [The agreement offered her $2,500 per year for the next six years, a total of $15,000.] I told them they could take it and stick it up their ass; that's exactly what I said."

Flo's friends have repeatedly expressed amazement that Flo would sign such an agreement, which has disappeared from the Wayne County (Detroit) Circuit Court records that otherwise detail Flo's various legal struggles. Flo's personal history, however, beginning with her discarded agreement with Milton Jenkins, had encouraged her to believe her signature on a document committed her to nothing.

A second interpretation of Flo's apparent willingness to sign such a career-killing agreement is that she had changed. The enthusiastic, optimistic, song-belting, fighting Flo Ballard had lost ground to a newly emerging aspect of her personality: Flo the Fatalist, who pretended to be above it all but found it normal for her situation to go from bad to worse. This characteristic—feigned, short-term indifference coupled with long-term fatalism—also came to the fore when she did not speak up loudly to contradict the official version of why she was leaving the group: that she needed to rest. Had she done so, sympathy from her many fans might well have led to her immediate return to the Supremes or, more likely, an immediate placement in another group, either Motown or non-Motown.

Mary Wilson has described Roshkind sarcastically as "Motown's newest expert in public relations"; but assuming he was wearing his executive hat rather than his public relations hat that day, he did a good job for his corporate masters. He also did a good job for Diana Ross: not surprisingly,

Roshkind's chief task at Motown at the time was to guide and shepherd her career.

This agreement Flo signed would be the basis of many of her problems after she left the Supremes. As always, up to that point, Flo had no legal counsel advising her either before or during her meeting with Roshkind.

And just what kind of man was she facing? Four years after convincing Flo to sign the Motown release, Roshkind, according to the U.S. government, entered into an agreement with a company called California International Marketing Company (CIMCO) giving CIMCO the right to market a Motown oldies-but-goodies album titled *Motown 1964*, which included several songs featuring Flo. Without bothering to inform Motown, Roshkind suggested to CIMCO that all future disputes between Motown and CIMCO would be swiftly settled if CIMCO hired Roshkind's girlfriend, Dorothy Loeb, for promotional and public relations purposes in the selling of those albums, and paid her twenty cents for each album sold. On this basis, CIMCO paid Ms. Loeb $136,000 in 1972 and $99,300 in 1973. In court papers, the Feds said that Ms. Loeb never provided any public relations or promotional services for CIMCO. She did, however, marry Roshkind in 1973.

Roshkind did not report these payments on his tax returns. As a result, Roshkind, who by then was vice chairman of Motown Industries, was sentenced in 1978 to six months in jail for tax evasion. At his sentencing, he admitted guilt "without reservations and without qualifications." The judge sentenced him to serve his six months on furlough: he would be allowed to work at his regular job during the day and report to jail in the evenings. The judge also required that after Roshkind served his six-month "jail term," he serve twelve months in a community treatment center, leaving only for his employment and for three hours after each day's work. In addition, he required Roshkind to pay back taxes and penalties plus interest totaling about $250,000.

Still, Roshkind remained a respected figure in the music business in Hollywood. He left Motown Industries in 1980 and founded his own entertainment firm. And even though Motown then sued him for two million dollars for alleged breach of contract, Roshkind returned to Motown as a consultant in 1983. As Flo would say, "on and on . . ."

Motown and Roshkind apparently tried to sweeten the deal Flo made with Roshkind in 1967 by buying her a Cadillac, a plum rose El Dorado, at approximately the same time. "The car was paid for, cash," Flo said, "but I didn't pay for it. I don't know who paid for it. The only person I could think of that paid for the car was Motown. We even asked the dealer, and he wouldn't tell."

The possible gift of the Cadillac notwithstanding, the relationship between Flo and Motown at that point was touchy at best. Berry Gordy's siblings and Mary Wilson attempted to heal the breach. "Berry had another brother, Fuller Gordy, who was very nice," Flo said. "Gwen [Gordy] was also nice to me, but I'll never forget . . . Mary [Wilson] was in town and she was going to this party over at Berry's mansion house, so she said 'Well, why don't you go with me?' I said, 'No, no.' She was talking to Fuller on the phone, and Fuller said, 'Yeah, tell her she can come; I'll be glad to see her.'

The mansion Flo referred to was Gordy's palatial Detroit home. His growing wealth had been accompanied by steady improvement in his places of residence. When Motown was just beginning, he lived in an upstairs bedroom in one of the company's original buildings. As Motown made him richer, he moved into a series of middle-class houses in better and better Detroit neighborhoods. But these were tumbledown shacks compared with the luxurious mansion on Detroit's Boston Boulevard that Gordy purchased in 1967. The three-story house, unprepossessing from the street, had cost a million dollars to build in 1927. It had a central vacuum system, a marble-floored, marble-columned ballroom, a gymnasium, an Olympic-size swimming pool, a luxurious billiard room, a two-lane bowling alley, a private theater linked to the main house by tunnels, and an entire authentic pub, imported intact from England. Every room in the house was decorated with gold leaf, frescoed ceilings, and elaborate chandeliers. Gordy hung oil portraits of his friends and family in the entrance hall, including an oil painting of himself as Napoleon Bonaparte.

"So I went to the party," Flo said, "and I was sitting down, and I had on this long [hair] fall, and I felt somebody jerk it. I turned around—and Diane had pulled the fall. So I looked at her, and I told her don't do it again. So she ran over and told Berry I was trying to start something with her. He came over and told me, 'You have to leave; you weren't invited anyway.' . . . I remained sitting there, talking to Fuller. So Berry came back around and said to me, 'I thought I told you to leave, but since you haven't, I'll have you thrown out.' I'll never forget that as long as I live, and I say he's the most ridiculous man I ever met in my life. And Mary, she just broke down and just cried and cried; she said she just couldn't believe that he said that to me. She heard him say it, and she cried and she cried. And she said, 'If he's putting you out, then I'm leaving too. I don't want to be here either.' Even his brother Fuller said the same thing."

Not all the Motown parties Flo attended were downers for her. Later on, she attended a birthday party for one of Diana's daughters at the same Detroit mansion. When Diana sang "Happy Birthday" as part of the celebration, Flo remarked to a nearby reporter, "She's singing flat." For a moment, the old Flo had returned.

Indeed, Flo the Fighter was far from completely dead. After a month of thinking about the wounds that Motown had inflicted on her and the surrender agreement she had signed for Roshkind, she hired an attorney, Leonard Baun of the Detroit law firm of Okrent, Baun and Vulpe, to sue Motown, agreeing to pay him 20 percent of whatever he got from Motown for Flo. "Oh, he was rarin' to go, rarin' to go, ready to sue Motown," Flo said of Baun.

Motown made its first move one month later by giving Baun, as Florence's legal representative, the $75,689 that was being held by Motown in a joint Motown-Ballard account at Bank of the Commonwealth. On Baun's advice, Florence signed papers creating Talent Management Inc. (TMI) to run her future career, with Baun as president and treasurer. Baun immediately spent $5,000 of her money for Talent Management stock for himself.

Motown then released to Baun stocks that it had held in Flo's name. Baun used his own home address to apply for credit cards in Flo's name and his name. He used $10,003.39 of the trust fund to buy 341 shares of diversified growth stock and 343 shares of Dreyfus fund stock (the fund founded in part by Flo's former boyfriend's father) in Flo's name. And the next year, Baun paid himself $43,050.24 in attorney's fees, an amount much higher than his 20 percent fee agreement would seem to justify.

After taking care of these details, Baun made it his task to find out what else Motown owed Flo. Motown promptly threw up a cloud of dense legalese. The company's attorneys simultaneously denied that Flo had any contracts with Motown and argued that if she did, they could not be released. The company also said that she could audit the company's books at her own expense, but she didn't have the money to pay for such an expensive undertaking.

Finally, Baun and Flo, working with fragmentary information provided by the records Motown chose to release and with Flo's memory, concluded that the Supremes had grossed $1.6 million in 1967, out of which, in accordance with the Motown contract, hotel costs, traveling expenses, and recording expenses had all been paid. A Motown talent management subsidiary with which Flo had also signed a contract, again without benefit of an attorney's advice or counsel, had received 15 percent of her earnings off the top.

Although Baun wanted to sue, he and Flo tried to work out a settlement, incorporating the money Motown already had given Flo and what she believed Motown still owed her. Cynics would say that the costs of a suit, which Baun had pushed for, would have increased his fees immensely, but his supporters would say that a suit would have been the only way to obtain information from Motown showing how much the company truly owed the founding member of an immensely successful group such as the Supremes.

Flo's legal team was burdened with the additional need to determine Flo's income for 1965 and 1966, years in which she had not received any royalties.

Baun felt that Motown was so unforthcoming with information that he wrote Gordy directly about his problems in getting relevant information from the company. Unfortunately, all this did was incense Baun's negotiating partner at Motown, Ralph Seltzer, who was angered that Baun had gone over his head.

Motown's position was that it would not pay Flo anything other than the original fifteen thousand dollars, causing Baun to testify in a deposition related to the case that Motown was treating her "like a vassal." He described their position as "We don't owe you anything. We have paid you for what you have done up to now. That is the end of it."

The company's negotiating position was that Supremes records would not be big sellers in future years and that, simultaneously, determination of their future worth was not possible. Unfortunately, Baun accepted this argument. He was unable to foresee that Supremes tunes, in numerous forms, would remain big sellers for decades to come. In fact, Baun had little or no experience in entertainment law; he had spent his career as a personal injury lawyer.

Nearly as unforgivable was Baun's inability to come up with a value for the name "Supremes," the hottest recording group of all time. He said he knew it had goodwill value, "but to say how much it was worth or how hot it is, I didn't know." Much more accurately, one of Flo's future attorneys, Gerald K. Dent, called the "Supremes" name "a household word" and estimated its worth at one million dollars. Perhaps Baun was influenced by the unanimous denial by Motown executives that Florence had chosen the name "Supremes," although Diana Ross later admitted in writing that Flo had chosen the name and that in fact she had done so over Ross's objections.

Considering Baun's weak defense of his client's interests, it's no wonder that he and Motown were eventually able to agree on a settlement. The obvious alternative was for Flo to sue Motown, as Baun had originally suggested, but another factor was in play now, involving an ace that Motown had been storing up its sleeve. "Baun came back and told me," Flo said, "'Well, look, if I take it to court, Berry Gordy's going to say that you drink.'

"Me being young, I thought if the public read something about that, then they'd get the wrong impression," Flo said. "So Leonard Baun says Motown's offering a settlement for $160,000. . . . First he said $160,000, then he said $250,000. . . . But he did come over with some papers. OK, I trusted Leonard Baun, the attorney. I didn't know what the papers meant. I just signed them, and that was it. So I guess what I signed was a settlement, OK."

Like its predecessor, this new agreement prohibited Flo from using the name "Supremes" in her publicity and from suing Motown, Ross, Wilson, or Birdsong. It also closed the book on future royalties from past recordings, in effect cutting Flo off, in 1968, from all future revenue that would flow from the gold mine named "The Supremes." To settle all of Flo's claims against the company, Motown gave Baun a check for $160,000. He was also entrusted with the $300,000 worth of Flo's assets that Motown, after paying all the Supremes' expenses, had saved on her behalf.

13

"I Now Pronounce You"

I don't know why he appealed to me.

—Florence Ballard, on her husband,
Tommy Chapman

JUST DAYS AFTER signing her settlement with Motown, Flo married Thomas Chapman, who'd replaced Roger Pearson in her affections the year before. She had previously known the twenty-eight-year-old Chapman only as a fellow Motown employee. But as her relationship with Pearson ran down, she became romantically involved with the tall African American and began seeing him exclusively.

"I don't know why he appealed to me," Flo said of Tommy, and others have asked the same question. According to a woman who worked as a housekeeper for Flo and Tommy, their relationship had a violent side on at least one occasion. She said that once she "found Flo lying on the floor, with bruises on her legs. [Flo's mother] Lurlee came down from upstairs and told Tommy, 'If you hit her again, I'll kill you.'"

Perhaps Pat Cosby has the best explanation for Flo's attraction to Chapman. She noted that Tommy, although his position at Motown was much lower than Flo's, had talked with Flo as her equal. "She didn't have to be Flo Ballard of the Supremes with Tommy," Cosby said. "She could just be Flo. They had a man-and-woman relationship, not a man-and-one-of-the-

Supremes relationship," which could easily have described her relationship with Roger Pearson.

Chapman proposed to Flo by phone from San Juan. After she accepted his proposal, he resigned from Motown and returned to Detroit. The couple then flew to Hawaii, where they were married in a civil ceremony on February 29, 1968. There were no guests. Mixing romance and business is never a good idea, and making preparations for a Hawaiian wedding and honeymoon while she was in the process of settling with Motown may have hindered Flo's ability to think clearly during her struggle to wrest her financial assets from Motown's grip.

Upon hearing of the impending marriage, according to Flo, Berry Gordy told Chapman that "he was making a big mistake because the marriage would never work." Gordy also told him, "If the marriage doesn't work, you can always come back and work for me."

While calling Tommy "very nice," former Marvelette Katherine Anderson Schaffner also said that at the time Tommy got involved with Flo, "Flo had problems with being out of the group, and Tommy thought there was money to be made." Others have contended that whenever Flo had money to spend, Tommy was around, but when she ran out of money, he never seemed to be there. Whatever the truth of this formulation, the newly married couple did establish a commercial as well as marital relationship: Flo appointed Tommy her business manager for what she hoped would become a successful solo career.

14

Dashed Hopes

It felt great to be recording again.

—Florence Ballard

FLO HAD REASON to be optimistic about her post-Motown career. Her negotiations with Motown had been conducted while she, Leonard Baun, and Chapman were focused on a promising opportunity for the ex-Supreme: ABC Records executives wanted Flo to sign with their company. They had insisted, however, that they could not offer her a contract unless she first settled with Motown.

While Flo may have been hoping that she could eventually resurrect her career without Motown's help, recent history suggested otherwise. Former Motown superstars such as Mary Wells had left the company and then dropped out of sight. After David Ruffin of the Temptations was expelled from the group, he was reduced to attending Tempts concerts, singing along with them from the audience, and then trying to jump up onstage to physically retake his place with his former group. His former colleagues had to hire extra security guards to keep him offstage. Another Temptation, Paul Williams, had sunk even further. Williams had been present at Flo's first audition with Milton Jenkins years before and had been the only person present at her second audition. In both cases he had encouraged her to continue her singing career and to form the Supremes as he continued his singing career and helped form the Tempts. But after decreasing his role in the Tempts due to illness, Williams committed suicide by shooting himself in the head in 1971 while sitting in a parked car only two blocks from Motown's Detroit headquarters.

Flo and Tommy had stressed to Baun that Flo "wanted to go into the performing artist field as an individual," Baun would later testify. He said that he, Flo, and the rest of her team were worried by the "fact that Motown was a very powerful factor in the performing artist field . . . and if we could not terminate the relationship on a more or less friendly basis, [Motown] might take, in some manner, adverse steps to actually impede her career." When Baun was asked, in a court deposition, "You mean like blackball her?" he replied, "It was obvious that Motown did have a lot of influence—that many of the established agencies booked for the performing artists who had contracts with Motown. . . . Mr. [Louis] Zito [an aide to Flo in her attempt to establish herself as an independent artist] told me that he had direct conversations with people in New York who felt that they did not . . . want to touch Flo because she was hot, because of what was, more or less, publicly known—that friction had developed between Ms. Ballard and Motown's organization."

Two booking agency employees had both told Baun that "they had apprehensions in trying to get bookings for Florence," Baun later testified. "They had received no threats. No one ever told me that, nor did anyone ever say that Motown had gone out of its way to impede Ms. Ballard's ability to perform as an individual. This was in the back of our minds that they [Motown] might try."

When Baun was asked if this was discussed with Motown during settlement negotiations, he responded, "Oh, yes, we talked about it, naturally. They always laughed it off and said, 'We wouldn't do anything to harm Florence. She is our friend.'"

Flo would have disagreed with this statement. She certainly didn't trust Gordy or Motown at this point and knew better than most the power that they wielded within the industry. And she wasn't the only one who viewed changing labels as risky. She alleged in 1975 that ABC president Larry Newton had told her, in her words, "'You know, it's not good to switch recording companies, because once you record for one company and go to another, it's not too good.'"

Uncertainties there may have been, but the ABC offer was genuine. Fate had given Flo another chance. Motown had given her a somewhat substantial sum and by arriving at a new settlement agreement had made it possible for Flo to sign with ABC Records, which she promptly did.

ABC at the time was a growing and popular record company, but, with the exception of Ray Charles, it had little or no experience with black artists. Among the popular groups on the label were the Mamas and the Papas and Three Dog Night. Even though Flo wasn't allowed to use the name "Supremes" in any future publicity, ABC clearly wanted her fame as a former Supreme, along with her marvelous voice, to diversify and strengthen its roster. What Flo wanted was a hard-charging record company to jump-start what she hoped would be a new career as a solo artist with a well-recorded, well-promoted hit.

"I said, 'OK, great,'" Flo said of the ABC offer. She flew to New York to sign the contract, along with Baun, Chapman, and former Motown public relations man Alan Abrams. Abrams had represented the Supremes when Flo was a member of the group, but he had been discharged by Motown on Pearl Harbor Day, December 7, 1966. Abrams said Motown executive Michael Roshkind, who fired him and was aware of the day's historic significance, had told him, "Consider yourself bombed." According to stories in the *Detroit Free Press*, Abrams was dismissed not for any fault of his own but because, partly owing to his own assiduous public relations work, the Supremes had become so successful that Motown then wanted the group to be represented by a nationally known PR firm.

Although an inveterate optimist, Abrams said he was discouraged about Flo's solo campaign from the beginning. He noted that constant indecision and missteps plagued the effort. Its symbolic start, he said, Flo's trip to New

York City, set the tone for all that happened later. At a March 6, 1968, meeting with ABC president Larry Newton in a restaurant, where Flo was to sign her ABC contract, the businessmen and public relations people at the table paid more attention to a nearby table where a group of coeds from Vassar or Smith were interviewing ageless superstar Myrna Loy, Abrams said. (Ironically, Ms. Loy was always a champion of African American actors and their right to be treated with dignity.)

Nevertheless, Flo signed the exclusive recording contract with ABC. The contract covered the two following years but allowed either party to drop out without penalty after year one.

In the spring of 1968, when all seemed possible, Flo recorded some sessions at ABC's New York studios. "It felt great to be recording again," she said; "it really felt great. I really liked it a lot." She noted that ABC had hired "these three girls to do background; they were really good too, very good. And the music, they had gotten a band, session men, musicians who play for records."

The sessions were produced by George Kerr and resulted in two songs for ABC: "It Doesn't Matter How I Say It (It's What I Say That Matters)," a Motown sound–type of tune, and Flo's version of the Little Anthony and the Imperials' song "Goin' out of My Head."

"I liked the tunes, sure did, and my voice hadn't declined. The records sound great to me, and to a lot of people," Flo said.

She had a major complaint, however. "The company released the record, but they just wouldn't push it."

This is the kind of situation in which an experienced business manager was needed, and there is no question that one could have been found to take the post from Flo's husband. Any seasoned manager would have dealt swiftly with a record company that underpublicized Florence Ballard, if by no other means than threatening to denounce the company in the media for ignoring Flo's potential as a very recent Supreme and threatening to immediately take her elsewhere. But Tommy Chapman was out of his depth in this role, even though Flo and Baun had incorporated him as Talent Management, Inc., with Flo as his sole client. His only business experience up to that time had been as a low-level Motown employee.

In one of the most pathetic episodes in Flo's career of dramatic ups and downs, Tommy's reaction to ABC's failure to publicize her new tunes was to carry around a box full of her recordings to place in record shops and give to DJs. WCHB in Detroit began to play it, but the record never moved up the charts.

After the failure of these first two tunes, ABC brought in Robert Bateman, the experienced former Motown producer who had been present at the Supremes' first Motown audition and who had noticed Diana Ross's habit of singing through her nose. Flo once again journeyed to ABC's New York studios, and she and Bateman went right to work. Flo sang fourteen tunes, which Bateman recorded.

ABC then released two of the tunes on a second 45. On one side was the song "Love Ain't Love," written by vibrant disco songsmith Van McCoy. On the flip side was a tune Bateman had written for Flo, "Forever Faithful." For many of Flo's fans, this poignant song became the symbol of her long decline, partly because its name seemed to refer to Flo's refusal to denounce Gordy and Ross when the topic of her dismissal from the Supremes was newsworthy and when a denunciation might have helped increase her celebrity.

The records were released, but, in Flo's words, "That was it. Anybody can put out a record." What she meant was unless a record is pushed, no one will play it. Although "Love Ain't Love," in Author Randall Wilson's words, "revealed the power and range of Flo's voice," without a major publicity effort from ABC, few DJs loved it enough to play it.

After the unsuccessful release of "Love Ain't Love" / "Forever Faithful," the company dropped its renewal option on Flo's two-year contract with the company and effectively washed its hands of her. If Motown had done the same with Flo, Mary, and Diane immediately after the failure of "Who's Loving You? / Buttered Popcorn" in 1962, the Supremes would be remembered today only by a few musicologists as the third pop group of that name to go under forever.

As for the album for which Flo had recorded the rest of the fourteen songs, *You Don't Have To*, ABC simply dropped it. "I began to get the message," Flo said. "'Flo, your recording contract with ABC is not going nowhere.'" In any case, she said, "It was a yearlong contract [with a one-year renewal option], because I said I wouldn't get tied up no more for a lot of years. It was fine with [ABC president Larry] Newton, because he wasn't interested anyway, evidently."

Despite Flo's fame in Detroit as a former Supreme, many DJs outside Detroit were not familiar enough with the name "Florence Ballard" to give her first record the play she deserved. Many of them might have been encouraged to do so by a wave of publicity about the record from Detroit, reminding them that she was a former Supreme, but the *Detroit Free Press* and the *Detroit News* were in the middle of a long strike. In those pre-Internet days, this meant that very little news of any kind was emanating from the Motor City. The records died, virtually stillborn.

Flo and her entourage tried to boost the records' sales through concerts and touring, but Chapman's lack of experience hurt Flo here as well. The sites at which the new, solo Flo would be allowed to perform were poorly chosen.

In the summer of 1968, for instance, Flo was booked to play at the Wonder Garden in Atlantic City. Tony Turner wrote in his book *All That Glittered: My Life with the Supremes* that it was shocking to see her there, where prostitutes and pimps made up the bulk of the audience. While waiting to perform at this high-class joint, Flo was staying at the Hotel Traymore. A long time before, the Traymore had been the place to stay in Atlantic City, but now it smelled musty, the drapes were in shreds, and roaches crawled up and down the walls.

When Turner asked Flo what she was going to sing, she said she didn't know. Turner, who had known the Supremes when they were at the top and wrote a book about his time with them, couldn't believe her answer. A diva coming unprepared to a scheduled performance? Then he discovered that although Flo had arrived with costumes, staging, and a whole show put together, the band at the Wonder Garden couldn't read music. Flo was forced to wait to decide which songs she would sing while a representative of the house band wrote down on a brown paper bag a list of the songs everyone in the band knew and she figured out which of those songs *she* knew. Management insisted that Flo not start her show until the place was full, and there were no dressing rooms, forcing Flo to arrive at the club fully dressed and wait in the manager's office until it was time to go on. Onstage, she was lit only by individual red and white light bulbs. An attendant clicked them on when she went onstage and clicked them off when she left the stage. According to Turner, after the show, a hooker came backstage with a bottle of cheap champagne, blurted out, "Flo, you deserve better," and burst into tears.

Responding to Turner's account, Abrams argued that before gambling was legalized in Atlantic City, every hotel there could be termed a fleabag. He also said that the team finally decided to stop Flo's touring when she became too pregnant to continue.

Flo and Tommy were in fact expecting twins. Some women might not have wanted to have children at that point in their careers, but as Pat Cosby noted, "Having children was part of the woman Flo wanted to be." In any case, Flo could easily have returned to her career a short while after giving birth—had there been a career to return to.

There was not. Flo appeared on a few local television shows on the East Coast in an attempt to keep her career going. She also performed with Wilson Pickett, for whom she and the other Supremes had sung background before migrating to Motown. In September 1968, she joined Bill Cosby in a performance at the Ambassador Theatre in Chicago. Her spirits were lifted by the enthusiastic public response she received when she and Tommy rode with comedian Godfrey Cambridge in the largest African American parade in the United States, Chicago's annual Bud Billiken Parade. She also made a big splash at an inaugural function for President Nixon on January 20, 1969. But that was pretty much it. Flo's attempt to boost sales of her records through public performances and appearances had failed.

Baun blamed ABC for failing to coach and handle Flo correctly and find the right songs for her to record. Otis Williams of the Temptations said that "although there was no question that Flo had the voice to make it as a solo, the problem was that she didn't get the right material or the right direction."

However, in a world where publicity is all, or almost all, Flo's attempt at a solo career failed mainly because, according to the terms of her settlement agreement with Motown, Flo couldn't use the name "Supremes" to publicize her new records. Therefore, the release of each record became a test of how many people recognized her name when it wasn't linked with "Supremes." Flo might well have overcome this disadvantage if she had been able to re-create the Supremes sound on her records, but without two other female vocalists singing beside her in the roles she and Mary Wilson had so successfully filled, she couldn't do that. Some purist fans could argue that she would have also needed the Motown house musicians and the Motown studios, but it's possible that ABC could have saved Flo by rounding up background singers and starting a new group with a name reminiscent of the Supremes. Perhaps the Majestics? The Queens of Pop? The Primettes? The Dreamettes? There is not the slightest indication that such a scheme was ever considered.

And, although Flo was legally forbidden to use the name "Supremes" in her own publicity, there was nothing to prevent DJs from referring to her as "former Supreme Flo Ballard." The mind boggles to think what fun many DJs could have had, and what publicity they could have drummed up, if two "Supremes" groups—the "real" Supremes starring Diana Ross and Mary Wilson, and the "other real Supremes" starring Florence Ballard—both produced records simultaneously for a significant period. The two groups would undoubtedly have been seen as competing in a "Battle of the Supremes."

Scherrie Payne would come up with a similar idea in 1986. By then herself a former Supreme, she formed the singing group "Former Ladies of the Supremes," very significantly called FLOS, which at various times included not only Payne but by then former Supremes Jean Terrell, Cindy Birdsong, and Lynda Laurence. It's tempting to think that not only ABC but also Motown lost a major opportunity by not trying something like this. But we'll never know what might have been. ABC Records, lacking imagination, lacking a tradition of developing its own musicians, and lacking a quick hit from the Lost Supreme, merely kicked the fallen Flo to the curb.

Flo's alter ego in the *Dreamgirls* movie, Effie Melody White, resuscitates her music career in part by performing solo at a small Detroit club and putting out a solo record, "One Night Only," on a small label. The song is soon covered by the Dreams, the film's version of Diana Ross and the Supremes. Finally, the Diana Ross character forces the Gordy character to put out Flo's original recording, apparently ensuring her solo stardom. In the real world, happy endings are rarer than they are in Hollywood, and none of the above occurred.

15

Fleeced Again

Where in the hell the check went I'll never know.
I never saw it.

—Florence Ballard

FLO'S CAREER WITH ABC produced nothing except two records that didn't sell and an album that wouldn't be released until long after she died. Adding insult to injury, she never received the advance that ABC had promised her. ABC had agreed to pay her $15,000 when she signed her contract, but "Where in the hell the check went I'll never know. I never saw it," Flo said. "Leonard Baun picked it up some kind of way or something. And when I asked Leonard Baun, he said he got it. . . . I don't know what happened to the $15,000 check or how it was cashed, for that matter."

Baun had also never given Flo the money Motown had given him, as Flo's legal representative, under the second separation agreement. "They sent the settlement check to Leonard Baun, and Leonard Baun cashed the check and used the funds," Flo said. "I never received the settlement check."

When Flo returned home after giving birth to her twin girls, Michelle and Nicole, on October 13, 1968, Baun, who had been entrusted with the management of Flo's $160,000 just eleven months before, told her that all the money he had received on her behalf from Motown and from ABC had been spent. What should have been the start of a career-reviving year for Flo turned to ashes. On March 17, 1969, Flo, in a state of shock and accompanied by her brother Billy, went to Baun's office and demanded that he return all her documents to her so that she would at least have a chance to determine what had happened to all her earnings from her Supremes years, as well as her ABC advance. Baun gave her some of the documents but refused to give her others. On April 2, Flo fired him as her attorney and sent a copy of his termination letter to the Wayne County Prosecutor's Office.

Flo and Billy spent the next year trying to find another attorney to sue Baun. Baun called the accusation that he had mismanaged Flo's money ridiculous and was quoted as saying, "She will be flat broke after she pays her taxes."

To say the least, Flo found this difficult to believe. But when she tried to find someone in power to help her, she was turned away at every attempt. Essentially, she was trying to find one attorney to attack another in a way that would certainly damage and possibly destroy the attacked attorney's career, and possibly the attacking attorney's career as well.

Flo and Billy also tried to interest the Wayne County Prosecutor's Office in prosecuting Baun. A Detroit police lieutenant named Boggs told them he would investigate the matter but never got back in touch with Billy or Flo. Infuriated, Flo wrote the police department's Citizen Complaint Bureau the next month and received a reply saying she and Billy should insist on an appointment with the assistant county prosecutor, Jay Nolan, to discuss Flo's complaint against Baun. But Nolan said he would have to disqualify himself from the case because he knew Baun. He suggested that the Michigan State Bar would be the proper forum for Flo's complaint, and the next month Flo filed a complaint with the Bar's Grievance Board.

Later that month, however, impatient, nearly out of money, and fearing that the wheels of justice would grind so slowly that she would be living on the street before receiving recompense, Flo paid a $200 advance to attorney O. Lee Molette to obtain the missing money and papers from Baun. Molette soon decided he could not or would not handle the case. Shortly thereafter, Flo paid another $200 retainer to attorney Joseph Louisell. A few days later, according to court papers filed later by Flo, Louisell "told me that Mr. Baun was his neighbor and that he would go over to Mr. Baun's house to get my money and files. After hearing this I requested that he send my retainer back." Louisell did so, and Flo then contacted two other lawyers, who, she said, declared the case too big for them: Freddy Burton and an attorney named Bloom.

During her search, Flo said, one attorney told her, "'Leonard Baun and I are good friends. I can't possibly do anything.' They wouldn't prosecute him or anything. So that's when I said as far as I'm concerned they're all down there holding hands, and I felt that all my rights were just violated."

Flo, Tommy, and Billy finally got an appointment to see Wayne County assistant prosecutor Mike Connors on May 29, 1969. After arriving at the meeting place and waiting forty-five minutes, they concluded he would not show up for the appointment. The three wandered over to the courtroom run by Wayne County Circuit Court judge George W. Crockett Jr., a fellow African American, where assistant prosecutor William O. Cain, presumably prompted by the judge, referred Flo to attorney Bernard Adams.

It's appropriate that Flo, Tommy, and Billy went to Judge Crockett's courtroom when they became desperate for succor. Crockett had cofounded what is believed to be among the first racially integrated law firms in the United States. As manager of the Mississippi Project during the civil rights struggle, he had personally attempted to find the men who had murdered civil rights workers James Chaney, Andrew Goodman, and Michael Schwerner. As a Detroit judge, he became involved in the New Bethel Baptist Church shootout in which a Detroit police officer died and more than 140 African Americans were arrested. And finally, in the House of Representatives, which he entered at age seventy, he became well known for his constant denunciations of apartheid in South Africa.

Shortly after meeting with Crockett, Flo hired Adams as her attorney, and he started negotiating with Baun, who refused to give up the documents involved.

Over the next six months, Flo and Billy fruitlessly contacted the FBI, the State Attorney General's Office, the American Bar Association, the IRS, the Circuit Court, state senator Julian Bond, state senator (later, mayor of Detroit) Coleman Young, the Civil Liberties Union, Congressman John Conyers, five or six more lawyers, state representative James Del Rio (later a judge), and officials of the Bank of the Commonwealth. In continuing desperation, Flo also fruitlessly sent President Nixon a plea for assistance. Finally, on September 17, 1969, she signed a contract engaging the prestigious Detroit African American law firm of Patmon, Young, Kirk, Dent & Feaster as her legal representative against Baun. She asked Patmon, Young to sue Motown as well. Believing that Motown hadn't given her anywhere near all the money she was due, she had nothing to lose, now that her solo career was dead, and everything to gain by jousting once again with one of America's largest black-owned firms.

Attorney Gerald Dent of Patmon, Young was assigned to both cases. He filed suit against Baun's law firm on Flo's behalf on October 1, 1970. In accusing Baun of "gross negligence, malpractice and breach of fiduciary duties and obligations," Flo and Dent charged that

- Motown had given Baun $75,689 that Motown owed Flo, which Baun had not turned over to Flo, and some of which Baun had used to purchase stocks and securities in his own name.

- Baun had induced Flo to create Talent Management International, Inc. to generate superfluous attorney fees for him and his law firm. She noted that Baun had had no previous experience in the music business, legal or otherwise.

- Baun, without Flo's consent, had utilized $5,000 of her trust funds to purchase stock in TMI, some of which he caused to be issued in his name; had become president and treasurer of TMI; and had commingled some of Flo's funds that had been entrusted to him with his own.

•

Baun had obtained possession of stock issued in Flo's name, buying without Flo's consent or knowledge $10,000 worth of stock with money from her trust fund.

•

Baun had paid himself $43,050.24 during 1968 in legal fees, some of this amount paid to other attorneys he had hired without Flo's knowledge or consent.

•

Baun had endorsed Tommy Chapman's name on a check made out to Chapman dated December 20, 1968.

In this and other ways, Flo claimed, Baun had withdrawn all the funds in the trust account and commingled them with his own funds. As a result of these activities, she charged, she suffered from a variety of mental and physical ailments.

Baun's partner Rudolph Vulpe, who had left the firm in 1967, was dropped from the case, but Baun's other partner, Harry Okrent, was not. Although there's no evidence that Okrent had anything to do with the alleged mistreatment of Flo, his status as Baun's partner—thus partly responsible for Baun's actions—would later cost him a substantial sum of money.

Baun denied the charges, contending that he had performed one thousand hours of legal work for Flo in 1967, 1968, and 1969, that his legal fees were reasonable, and that he had worked diligently on her behalf. He denied that he purchased any stock in his own name with Flo's money, but if he had, it was a mistake, and in any case the stock went into a joint bank account with Flo. Baun also struck a low blow by claiming that the reason Flo's ABC endeavor failed was that she "did not possess the talent necessary to make the venture a success." The suit began percolating through the courts.

Meanwhile, investigators and attorneys working for the Michigan State Bar Grievance Board had begun closing in on Baun for stealing more than $147,000 from the estates of four other people, all deceased and all unrelated to Flo. Baun would be found guilty of these charges by a hearing panel in 1975. Two members of the three-person panel would vote to suspend his license to practice law for two years, and the third would vote to disbar him. After hearing the panel's recommendation, the Grievance Board would vote unanimously to disbar Baun. Baun appealed to the courts, which would uphold the disbarment on April 21, 1976. Baun would appeal again in 1978, citing new evidence that during his period of misconduct he had been suffering from a massive brain tumor pressing upon both frontal lobes of his brain. At the hearing on this appeal, Baun's former law partner, Harry Okrent, would take the stand and undergo questioning.

BAUN'S ATTORNEY: *Did you notice any change in [Baun's] attitude, his behavior, his appearance, anything of that nature?*

OKRENT: *Very sudden change.*

ATTORNEY: *Sudden?*

OKRENT: *Very sudden. I can almost pinpoint the day. It would have been either December of 1968 or January of 1969 [just after Flo's attempt to build a solo career had collapsed].*

ATTORNEY: *What brings you to that date?*

OKRENT: *Because all of a sudden the big, friendly, puppy dog became a surly dog. He didn't seem to enjoy anything. He had a sort of crazy, almost immediate big-shot complex. He became enamored in trying to be a talent seller of people that have artistic talent of one sort or another. Show business intrigued him. The law business, he worked at it, but it was obviously work, it wasn't play anymore.*

Despite Harry Okrent's testimony, Baun's appeal was rejected and he would remain disbarred until 1981.

16

Bleak House

*Within the plantation system, you don't
really resist.*

—Attorney Gerald Dent, on
Motown Records

IN ADDITION TO working on Flo's case against Leonard Baun, her new attorney, Gerald Dent, filed suit on her behalf against Motown, as well as Gordy, Ross, Wilson, and Birdsong on February 1, 1971. The naming of her fellow Supremes—particularly Wilson and Birdsong—in the suit was largely pro forma; everyone knew it was aimed primarily at Motown and Gordy.

The suit charged that the defendants had conspired to separate Flo from her royalties. It also charged that Gordy and Ross had "secretly, subversively and maliciously plotted and planned" to expel Flo from the group. It noted that Flo had arrived at a settlement with Motown on February 22, 1968, for a total of $139,804.94 in rights and royalties, a sum that was "meager and grossly inadequate." Although Gordy had posed as her "trusted friend," she argued, Motown and its talent management arm, International Management Company, also headed by Gordy, had kept the $4 million in royalties she was owed.

Flo said in her suit that she had received a $225 weekly allowance but had never seen an accounting of the Supremes' income. Based on this lack of information, she requested that her earlier agreement with Motown, which forbade her to bring future suits against anyone or anything related to the Supremes or Motown, and in which she had signed away her rights to any future income from the Supremes, including royalties from records she sang on, be declared nonbinding.

Michael Roshkind also was a defendant in the suit, which asked for the $4 million in royalties, plus $4.5 million in punitive damages. Flo also claimed other relatively minor damages totaling another $200,000. And finally, as the stinger on the end of the scorpion's tail, Florence asked the court to forbid the Supremes from using the name "Supremes," partly because she had selected it in the first place but had been denied the right to use it.

Dent worked for two and a half years preparing and arguing this case against Motown. The problematic relationship between Motown and its performing artists was succinctly expressed by a courtroom exchange between Dent and the judge in the case, Wayne County Circuit Court judge Benjamin D. Burdick. Burdick questioned Dent about why Flo hadn't fought harder against the unfair compensation she had been receiving while she was a Motown star. The attorney replied:

DENT: *Within the plantation system, you don't really resist.*
JUDGE: *What do you mean by the plantation system?*
DENT: *Plantation system like in the Old South, the slave system and the servant system.*
JUDGE: *Do you mean the slaves didn't resist?*
DENT: *I'm talking about the relationship that existed.*
JUDGE: *Do you mean this was an "or else"?*
DENT: *It was.*
JUDGE: *"Do this or else?"*
DENT: *The situation was very similar to that. . . . It was her disposition not to fight them and the reason being that she was conditioned by this system and by Gordy and others to not offer any type of meaningful resistance to them in their particular ultimatum and ways.*

A respected attorney, Dent worked hard on the case, but in an amazing decision straight out of *Catch-22*, Judge Burdick would dismiss Flo's case in October 1971. His finding was that, because Flo had not given back the money she received after signing the original release "nor has offered to do so, nor has the monies in her possession, she may not maintain this suit against the defendants."

In other words, unless Flo returned to Motown the $160,000 settlement Motown had given to Baun, she could not seek what she was rightfully due from Motown. There was no way she could do this, as everyone involved knew, because her lawyer, Baun, had apparently embezzled most of the $160,000.

17

Friend or Foe?

*I Am the Master of My Fate. I Am the
Captain of My Soul.*

—from "Invictus," by William
Ernest Henley

FLO WASN'T THE only former Motown friend to turn foe.

After Tommy Chapman's disastrous handling of Flo's solo career, he went on to work at three Detroit food stores: Land O'Lakes, Bonnie's Bakeries, and finally, Borman's. "That was a good job; he worked there a good while," Flo said of his Borman's employment. But a new opportunity in the music business opened up in 1971, when attorneys at Patmon, Young, and Kirk "got Tommy a job at Invictus Records," a company set up by Motown's best songwriters, Holland-Dozier-Holland (H-D-H), after they left Motown in the late 1960s. "He was supposed to travel with groups such as Chairmen of the Board as a sort of road manager," Flo said.

"I told Tommy it was ridiculous to go to Invictus, because he was making more money at Borman's." Flo said. "Invictus was paying him maybe $185 every two weeks, which is nothing, and he was making close to $200 a week at Borman's."

Tommy's move to Invictus spiked Flo's growing paranoia that people—perhaps including Tommy—were in league against her, especially after she met a man who, as she said, "told me that Invictus was actually Motown. So I said, 'Well how could that be?' Then this girl in Honey Cone, Edna Wright, said, 'I'm singing with Invictus, but my contract is with Motown.' And I couldn't put all that together, and then afterwards I found out that the majority of employees they had at Invictus were ex-Motown employees."

Flo was wrong about Invictus being part of Motown. H-D-H had written twenty-six Top 10 pop songs for Motown from 1963 to 1967. But they were much less productive than usual in 1967 and soon left Motown. In 1970 they founded the Invictus and Hot Wax record labels and arranged to have them distributed by Capitol and Buddah* Records.

Founding these companies took a lot of work on H-D-H's part, most of it unreimbursed. They went to all this trouble because they wanted a share of the lucrative publishing royalties on the songs they wrote, which Gordy was not about to give them. Underlying this royalty dispute, however, was H-D-H's belief that *they* were the reason Motown was so successful. Even though they'd been well compensated, they had chafed under Gordy's rule. They felt strongly about their new company and founded it as a declaration of freedom from Gordy's overriding influence.

Shortly after H-D-H left Motown, Gordy sued them for $4 million for breaching their contract, hoping to get them back. They countersued for $22 million, claiming he had cheated them out of royalties and had taken advantage of their youth and inexperience to dupe them into signing inferior contracts. They asked the judge to void their contracts and give them the rights to their songs. What really stung Gordy was that H-D-H claimed credit for Motown's success. In a fine gesture of contempt, they also asked the judge to appoint a "receiver"—a court-designated official—to replace Gordy as head of his own company. This may have been going too far, but their argument

---

*The spelling of the name of this company was later changed to "Buddha."

wasn't much off the mark. Before H-D-H started writing songs for Martha & the Vandellas ("Heat Wave" and "Nowhere to Run") and the Four Tops ("Baby I Need Your Loving" and "I Can't Help Myself"), these groups had had no hits whatsoever. And we know what happened when H-D-H met the Supremes.

Gordy and H-D-H eventually settled this dispute out of court. The court jockeying revealed, however, that Motown had paid H-D-H about $20 million in songwriting (though not publishing) royalties. To this day, whenever a song written by H-D-H is played on the radio, H-D-H receives three to six cents, as well as sharing in the royalties on the sale of records, tapes, and CDs, which puts into perspective the small sum that Motown had paid Flo.

The Invictus-Motown brawl also produced a deposition by Michael Lushka, Motown's former executive vice president of marketing and sales, in which he said that between 1974 and 1977, he had picked up bags of cash from Motown's independent record distributors and delivered them in briefcases to top Motown officials in Los Angeles. He said Gordy was not one of these executives. In exchange for the cash, Lushka said, the distributors received free promotional records that were exempt from royalties.

"I'd go out two or three times a year and probably bring in, you know, a minimum of a half-million dollars for the year," Lushka testified. He said Motown used the cash to promote its products and that some of this promotional effort involved paying radio stations to play Motown records. Paying radio stations to play records, also known as payola, is illegal. If, for that and possibly other reasons, the executives who allegedly received the briefcases full of cash didn't declare it on their income tax returns, they were also violating federal income tax statutes. Motown's lawyers denied all the charges in court, pointing out that no evidence to support Lushka's story had ever been presented.

Flo's lawyers may have reasoned that although her husband's move to Invictus didn't make sense financially, it certainly made sense psychologically. By taking a job with Invictus, Gordy's personal chauffeur and "lackey," as Flo put it, had become an employee of the company that was also accused of stealing Gordy's best songs. Not only that, H-D-H's desertion of Motown and formation of Invictus had weakened the new incarnation of the Supremes in particular. And the Supremes had also been weakened by the loss of Tommy's wife, Flo Ballard. Gordy was now facing what may have appeared to him to be an organized cabal: Flo and H-D-H, who could easily be seen as the missing muscle in his now declining company, plus Tommy Chapman.

At Invictus, H-D-H produced several hits, including "Give Me Just a Little More Time" by Chairmen of the Board, "Somebody's Been Sleeping" by 100 Proof (Aged in Soul), and "Band of Gold" by Freda Payne. (Payne's sister, Scherrie Payne, later became a Supreme as the group ran through a long series of post-Flo personnel changes.) Gordy suspected (but was never able to prove) that Holland-Dozier-Holland had written these tunes while still employed at Motown, had failed to give them to any Motown groups, and had then taken the tunes with them to their new company.

Significantly, however, Invictus produced only one #1 hit on the Pop charts, "Want Ads" by Honey Cone, limiting the company's record sales. The rest were hits but on the less lucrative Rhythm and Blues charts, showing that H-D-H were less interested than Gordy was in selling to white record buyers or less motivated to do so without the hit-obsessed Gordy on their backs.

Also, perhaps reacting to Gordy's insistence that Motown not release a song that Gordy did not think was perfect, Eddie Holland, after founding Invictus, let his writers and producers record whatever they liked, and if the resulting tune went nowhere, said only, "I told you so."

Because H-D-H hadn't learned other lessons Gordy had learned early on, including how to avoid the clutches of the big record companies, they were unable to prevent their bigger partners, Capitol and Buddah, from gobbling such a large slice of their revenue that Invictus found it very difficult to be consistently profitable.

While H-D-H hadn't inherited Gordy's ability to engage in penny-pinching when it mattered, Dozier had inherited Gordy's expansive grandiosity. He wanted the struggling Invictus to start producing movies and plays. The Holland brothers were reluctant to enter such risky and costly arenas while they were still having trouble making money from the records they produced. Dozier then abandoned ship for ABC.

Ironically, the Holland brothers, disgusted with the difficulties posed by life on the outside, returned to Motown in 1975, and Gordy welcomed them back in spite of their legal squabbling. Gordy may have admired the great songwriters for the same reasons he admired Diana Ross: they did not bother to hide their ambition and fought strenuously for what they wanted. The Holland brothers remained at Motown for only a few years though, before becoming independent producers once again.

18

Paranoid, Isolated, and Homeless

At various periods of time, Ms. Ballard has experienced distressful and abnormal amounts of fear and apprehension regarding people, causing her to manifest, at different times, paranoid tendencies.

—Attorney for Flo Ballard

CLOSING IN ON thirty years old, Flo had been an ex-Supreme for five years now. She continued to fight for what she felt was due her, but the battle was taking a terrible toll mentally, physically, and financially. And with the birth of her third child, Lisa, on July 15, 1972, her responsibilities increased.

On April 3, 1973, less than eighteen months after the dismissal of Flo's suit against Motown, a tragic incident would shock Flo and alter her legal team. Her attorney, Gerald Dent, was taking part in a hearing on a case unrelated to Flo's when he received two phone calls that seemed to disturb him. The contents of these calls were never revealed, but shortly thereafter Dent pulled a snub-nosed .38 revolver out of his briefcase. What he intended to do with it was not clear. Some have speculated that he was planning to display the revolver to demonstrate something having to do with the case. But the judge presiding over the case claimed that Dent first pointed the gun at

135

his own head, then aimed it at the judge, then aimed it at the police officer on the witness stand. At least twenty gunshots were fired. The judge said that Dent had begun the firing. Five bullets, fired either by the police officer on the stand, who was wearing his firearm while testifying, or other police or court officers in the room, hit the thirty-six-year-old Dent. He died instantly.

Florence was even more shocked by this incident than was the general public. Nevertheless, she continued as a client of Patmon, Young, which assigned attorney Donald Tate to represent her in appealing the dismissal of her $8.7 million suit against Motown.

Flo and Patmon, Young were partly successful. The Michigan Court of Appeals, although upholding the dismissal of her economic case against Motown, ruled on May 23, 1973, that she could still sue in a lower court for the emotional distress she claimed the record company and others had inflicted upon her.

The "emotional distress" Flo claimed in her lawsuit was no ploy. The collapse of her recording career and the theft of almost all of her funds had sent her into a downward spiral from which it looked like she'd never recover. Since 1969 she had begun spending all her daylight hours in her house, taking care of her daughters, cleaning and shopping but doing little else except watching television. Her marriage had suffered.

"Me and Tommy had some disputes, and we separated and I filed for divorce," Flo said. "Tommy countersued; he refused to let me get the divorce, because, he said, I wasn't in my right mind. Which maybe I wasn't. It just seemed like I was mad at the world. It seemed like I was mad at Tommy because he had worked for Berry. So I was putting the blame on him. I was saying, 'You worked for Berry; you probably still do work for Berry.' I don't know, it was all crazy. I began to get to the point where I was paranoid. I didn't trust anybody."

Flo possibly was paranoid, but there's some support for her view regarding Tommy's activities. Shortly before the couple separated, *Detroit Free Press* entertainment editor Barbara Holliday had come over to interview Flo and her husband for the paper's Sunday magazine, and had found herself greeted with hostile words by Tommy each time she mentioned something even remotely negative about Berry Gordy. When, in a follow-up article, Holliday wrote that Tommy had deserted his family and implied that he had married Flo for her money, he sued the *Free Press* for a correction, an apology, and $10 million. The suit, filed in August 1969, was dismissed for lack of progress in October 1970. Whatever the *Free Press* said about Tommy, he and his wife had badly needed the press at that time to advance his wife's struggling career. He was her business manager, and a manager with his client's interests at heart would have done anything to keep the Detroit media on her side.

Nevertheless, Flo and Tommy retained some affection for each other. After she filed for divorce in 1972 and he contested it, they "got together again," Flo said, "and started talking and decided to see if we could really make it. So we tried it for a while; then finally I said, 'Get out.' I began to take my anger out on him. I felt so much anger and hate inside because of what had happened to me until I just took it out on him. He left again, and then he came back again. When he came back the first time he stayed three months. That Christmas was one of the happiest the kids had had in a long, long time because he brought them everything that Christmas, everything they wanted. We were really happy. Then, after Christmas, the pressure, the strain—I just took out my hate, my anger, my feelings all on him. And I guess nobody likes that. So he left again."

Flo was not exaggerating the shift in her personality. In court papers her attorney noted that her plunge from fame and wealth to poverty and despair, with three young daughters to feed and an absent husband, "had caused a severe and painful personality change." He wrote that her personality "has changed from a very congenial nature to one that causes her at different and various periods of time to be extremely nervous, highly irritable at the slightest and imaginary provocation." Moreover, the lawyer wrote, Flo had gone from a person possessing "an outgoing, pleasant personality to one where during various periods of time she lapses into an extreme state of withdrawal from society, into herself," and manifested, at times, "paranoid tendencies."

Flo began having trouble making the house payments. Tommy provided child support for their three daughters, but it wasn't enough to cover the mortgage as well.

"At first I was told that the house was already paid for by Motown, by Berry Gordy," Flo said. "Then I found out that it wasn't paid for. So I kept trying to keep the house payments going. Tommy would bring money by for food and stuff like that, but when I said, 'What about the house note?' he said, 'Well, you're divorcing me, I don't have any place to stay; I have to pay my rent.'" By now, Tommy didn't have a job. "Invictus started laying off people in 1973, and he was one of them," Flo said. "So I said, 'I'll borrow it from somewhere,' but I never did. I asked Patmon, Young if they would help me to catch up on the back payments, which were $700 a month, and they said they couldn't. When I got the notice that I was losing my house [also in 1973], that really did it. I said, 'I can't even keep my house.'"

Trying desperately to avoid eviction, Flo pawned her jewelry, but finally she was notified by the bank that foreclosure was imminent. According to Mary Wilson, "Flo then went to another recording artist, who agreed to lend her $700. When she went to the artist's business office to pick up the money, she was told to sign an agreement outlining the method and amount of the repayment and several blank sheets of paper." She wisely refused to sign but received no money from the artist.

"Why my house?" she cried to friends. "Why couldn't I at least keep my house?" To Flo and the other Supremes, owning a home meant security. It was also a symbol of success. When the bank finally foreclosed, Flo and her three children moved into the small house occupied by Flo's sister Maxine and Maxine's five children.

Still, Tommy and Flo stayed together as best they could. "Tommy couldn't move with me because there was no room for him." Flo said. "And his own place was too small for us. It was just a little bitty apartment. He asked me and the children to move in with him, but I said no because it's too small. But he would come over and visit all the time, and we would go to the show and take the kids places, and we wound up back together." She was pro-Tommy throughout her life.

When the kids were asleep at night, Mary Wilson has written, Flo would make herself up, put on what was left of her finery, and drive around Detroit for hours, singing along to tapes in her car. Many nights she would drive by her old house, which had not been resold and was boarded up and vacant, and stare at it with longing.

Soon enough, that pleasure was denied her as well, when she lost her car. She had traded her plum rose El Dorado for a gold Fleetwood but sold it "because I couldn't afford to buy beds and stuff like that for my children. And I said, 'What's the sense of me having a car and my children don't have the right beds?' Plus they didn't have any toys, so I sold the car and bought them everything they wanted."

19

Three into Two Won't Go

It's much easier to keep a losing team together than a winning team. Winners develop personalities.

—Samuel Pearson, as quoted by his son Roger

WHILE FLO WAS being stripped of her money and her physical and emotional health, the post-Ballard Supremes weren't doing so well either. Flo Ballard and the Supremes had recorded ten #1 hits. The new "Diana Ross and the Supremes" scored only two: "Love Child" and "Someday We'll Be Together."

By contrast, the charts during that time, as far as other Motown artists were concerned, could have been ripped from *Billboard* of three or four years before. At one point, Marvin Gaye was at the top with "I Heard It Through the Grapevine" and Stevie Wonder was just behind him with "For Once in My Life." The Supremes were nowhere, however, sliding down the other side of the mountain of creativity and popularity that they had climbed with the help of Flo's strong voice and boundless enthusiasm. Gordy's feud with H-D-H hadn't helped either.

Tensions among the new Supremes lineup skyrocketed as record after record failed to ignite. This was exactly the opposite of what Gordy and Ross wanted. Their plan was to make Diana a solo act, but everyone agreed that

Diana could not walk away from a group that was struggling to stay alive. If she did, she would be seen as publicly deserting it in its moment of need. Nevertheless, Diana continued to distance herself from Mary and Cindy onstage.

"The Supremes were dying, and Motown was desperately trying to hide the fact," Tony Turner wrote. Now-forgotten Supremes recordings such as "The Composer" and "The Weight" failed to lift the group from the pits. The Supremes, formerly always perfectly coiffed and gowned for their stage appearances, started wearing whatever street clothes they happened to have on for their shows outside big cities. For the formerly stylish group, this was the equivalent of screaming, "Help us! Help us!" at the audience. These world-class vocalists had, unbelievably, returned to their "no-hit Supremes" status.

In the midst of all this, Motown's publicity department got too far ahead of itself, and the buzz began about Diana leaving the group to go solo. *Look* magazine did the first major story on the subject, a cover story titled "The Supreme Supreme" in what would become the last issue of *Look* ever published.

Gordy scrambled for a solution. He had planned to start Diana's solo career with a tune he thought would be a big success, "Someday We'll Be Together," a song that had been recorded by another group ten years earlier. But realizing that the theme and the sound would be perfect as the Supremes' break-up anthem, he had it released as the group's finale.

Although Gordy had lost much of his genius for songwriting and record production since becoming the name of the game fifteen years previously, he was right about "Someday"'s hit potential. As the record headed hitward, eventually reaching #1, Gordy and Motown announced the upcoming "Farewell Concert of Diana Ross." The famed singing trio, half-dead without Flo and almost totally dead without Cindy and Mary's full participation, gathered all its remaining strength and launched Diana as a solo performer at their final show together on January 14, 1970, at the Frontier Hotel in Las Vegas.

Intriguingly, David Ruffin's later attempt to change the name of the Temptations to "David Ruffin and the Temptations" took a much different course than Diana's rocky but eventually successful attempt to make herself the titled leader of the Supremes and then use the group as a launching pad for her solo career. This was ironic given the Supremes' and the Temptations' long history together at Motown.

Ruffin called a meeting of the group one day and said he wanted the Temptations to be known from then on as "David Ruffin and the Temptations." According to Otis Williams, in his book *The Temptations,* Ruffin told his singing partners that he was the dominant lead singer, and it was time he got his due.

"But this wasn't just any group," Williams wrote. "This was the Temptations, and no lead singer, no matter how great, would ever be set apart from the group." He told Ruffin, "Oh no, you can forget [the name change idea]. . . . We are not changing to no 'David Ruffin and the Temptations.' It's going to be 'the Temptations,' and that's it."

If Flo and Mary had been able to unite in this way against Diana early on, and if Gordy had been on their side, the history of the Supremes would have been much more like the history of the Temptations, and Flo might have been a singing star into the twenty-first century.

Ruffin's motive for trying to rename the group was the same as Diana's. Williams said Ruffin's mood was "a mix of arrogance and insecurity" and refers to "the desperation behind his cockiness." Possibly in Ruffin's case, and certainly in Ross's, both had been convinced since youth that they must become superstars and spent their lives working toward this goal.

After Diana's departure from the Supremes, Gordy replaced her with singer Jean Terrell, the sister of fighter Ernie Terrell, whom she had accompanied in the group Ernie Terrell and the Heavyweights. So the upheaval among the Supremes continued. But while Flo was undoubtedly interested in the fate of the group she had founded, she had more pressing concerns at this point in her life, as her own situation went from very bad to even worse.

20

Down, Down, Down and Out

I almost forgot who I was or what I had been.

—Florence Ballard

As Flo's career, her legal offensive, and her marriage all crumbled in the early 1970s, she began to drink and walk at night, "not knowing where I was going. It was like I was in a daze, just walking. It was like I didn't care anymore, I had given up.

"I began to go into a complete depression, where I would just withdraw from people completely, just stayed locked inside, wouldn't come out. I just didn't want to be seen or anything. . . . I guess I was drinking because I wanted to feel happy. But that only made it worse."

Her brother Billy probably didn't help Flo's mental state when he began to tell her that Motown and Baun had been acting together against her. "He began to say it was a conspiracy," Flo said. "Leonard Baun was like with Motown, and they were shuffling things back and forth. In other words, Motown was paying him money, saying the hell with her."

Billy, Flo said, "felt like so many people were involved in it. I began to think that they were, too. Then I began to get scared, scared to go outside. I don't know why, I just had a fear. Nobody had threatened me or anything;

I just had a fear . . . I got that way because I was out of the group, because I couldn't understand what was going on, because I wanted to find out about my money and couldn't.

"While drinking and walking, I kept saying, 'The money's gone, the house is gone, and the car is gone. I just don't care anymore.' And I didn't. I thought about suicide and a whole bunch of things."

Some of Flo's thoughts were about the people who had her money, and were presumably enjoying it, while she sank further into misery each day. "Leonard Baun had over $500,000 of my money. I don't know how he got a hold of that money. And somebody still has those stocks, and someone is also cashing my royalty checks to this day," she said. "But I don't know who, and I haven't been able to find out, so I guess I never will. The checks are being made out in my name, 'Florence Ballard,' and somebody's cashing them. There was somebody working at Motown, before they left Detroit, who saw the checks nearly every week. They were made out in my name, stamped, and shipped off somewhere." Motown insiders say some were shipped off to the West Grand Boulevard Company, an entity Gordy controlled.

In fact, it was perfectly legal for Motown to keep Flo's share of Supremes royalties. She had signed away the rights to her royalties when she accepted the $160,000 settlement from Motown. By signing away her future royalties, Flo had denied herself a significant sum. Mary Wilson later told one author that she was earning $80,000 a year in Motown royalties.

During the summer of 1974, when all Flo could manage to do was think about her losses and walk in darkness, she suffered a further humiliation. Her sister gave her a birthday party at their brother's house in Detroit. "I could never drink hard alcohol anyway, whisky and stuff like that," Flo said. "I drank some vodka, and I just completely blacked out. But I decided I was going to walk the dog after the party, and I was picked up in this car, and I said, 'Oh my God, what will I do now?' And I had on my diamond rings. Two guys picked me up and pulled me into the car. We were in a vacant lot, and I just knew they were going to kill me.

"One of the guys got out, and he was in back of the car, and the other one was standing on the passenger side. And they had taken the rings off, and they were looking at the rings. While one was standing there looking at the rings, I looked around for the other guy, and I could see him in back of the car. And he heard me lock that side. The other ran around to the driver's side, and I hit that lock real fast. And I said, 'What do I do now?' I said, 'I can't go anywhere,' and then I looked down and saw the keys were in the ignition. And I said, 'I'll be—' and took off. One of the guys stood in front of the car, and I tried to drive him over; I tried to kill him, but he jumped out of the way. I don't know where I was to this day. I got back to the house and called the police, and the police looked and said, 'You must be some hell of a woman. You got their car.' I got their car, and the police picked them up. They didn't get the rings back, but I didn't worry too much about the rings, because I said, 'At least I'm alive.'

"One was on parole; he was just twenty-two. They denied everything, but the police said, 'How can you deny that you picked this woman up when she has your car?' And they said, "A friend had it.' So the police said, 'Where's your friend?' They couldn't produce their friend. The police took both of them down and had them up in the lineup, and this one guy, about twenty-two, on parole, he couldn't see me, but I could see him. . . . I recognized him."

Flo, generous to a fault, forgave the man who had robbed her and might have killed her. She did not identify him to the police, and he was released.

Soon thereafter, she was mugged again. "One day I was walking to the store just around the corner to buy some beer," she said. "It was about four o'clock in the afternoon. I was walking down Santa Rosa—it was a pleasant cool day—all of a sudden somebody snatched my purse, and I was so shocked, I just dropped the beer. I thought maybe I should chase him, but he was gone so fast, I couldn't even see what he looked like. He was just short and black, looked like he had on gym shoes, so I guess that's why I didn't hear him. He was really flying. I came back home and called the police, but they couldn't find anything; and then about a week later they found my wallet on Buena Vista." Buena Vista was where Flo's house had been before she lost it.

"I had some identification with the Buena Vista street number on it, so whoever took it brought it back and threw it on that street," Flo said. "They took my marriage license, children's birth certificates, and voter's registration card. What they wanted with that, I'll never know. Maybe they just threw it away. The guy at the store found the door key in the alley, but we had changed the locks on the doors."

Flo found her lot increasingly dreary. Living in reduced circumstances "was very hard to accept," she said, "because I was used to shopping and buying the things I wanted. . . . I was used to living in a higher bracket of life.

"It seemed like things just began to crumble. I couldn't afford to buy any clothes for my children or buy anything new for myself, but the main part was I wasn't hardly able to pay my bills sometimes. That was really getting to me."

Squeezed in upstairs in Maxine's house with her three children while her finances crumbled, Flo finally suffered a mental breakdown. She was admitted to the psychiatric department of Henry Ford Hospital in Detroit in November 1974.

Although Flo's sister Geraldine took care of her family while Flo was hospitalized, "my kids suffered a lot," Flo said. "Even before I went into the hospital, they had worried looks on their faces. . . . They would wake up and see me crying, depressed, a lot of things."

Geraldine, Flo said, "had eight children, and with my three it was a packed house. My sister took very good care of them . . . but they were out of school, they were in a different environment, they didn't have me there, they didn't have their father there. I worried a lot about them in the hospital, and the doctor said, 'You really shouldn't worry, because you're going to have to get yourself together so you can always keep the children happy.' After that I didn't worry too much.

"I came out of the hospital and at that time I could no longer stay at my sister [Maxine's] house. It was too crowded. So I still didn't have anyplace else to go. Mary Wilson's mother had been talking to my mother and was asking about me and was told I didn't have any place to stay. So Mrs. Wilson said, "I didn't know that. Let her come here and stay." (Mrs. Wilson lived in Mary's house in Detroit.) "Then Mary called long-distance one day and told me to stay there as long as I wanted to—it was OK—which I thought was fantastic."

Living in the Wilsons' house was indeed a relief to Florence, but she needed to move again shortly in order to get her children back into the school they had been attending. "The kids were out of school . . . and I was worrying about that, worrying about that."

After about three weeks, the downstairs flat in her sister Pat's house became vacant, and Flo and her kids moved into it. They were soon joined by Flo's sister Linda and Flo's mother. The children returned to school, but she still worried about them. "They had to walk miles, looked like, all the way from Stoepel to Margarita, all the way down Livernois; that's like walking from Six Mile to Seven Mile," she said. "I had my foot in a cast from slipping on the ice, and I would stand in the window and cry every morning, it seemed like, because they looked so little and so alone in that long distance. And every day I'd just sit and worry until they got home."

The final straw came when Tommy finally stopped sending child support money. After that, "One day I was in the living room just lying on the sofa and my sister Maxine came over," Flo said. "She had been talking to my mother. Maxine said, 'Blondie, you need help. You're going to have to go on ADC or something. You can't go on like this.'"

Aid to Dependent Children (ADC) was the major welfare program of the day. Although reluctant, Flo applied to the program. She soon began receiving $135 every two weeks. Although the money helped, it left her with a deep sense of shame.

"I'd always been independent, ever since the age of fifteen. I'd always worked at babysitting and stuff like that, and then I got involved in singing. I was always doing something to make money for myself. Being on ADC after making all that money was a hard blow. I began to feel like I was just a lazy woman who didn't want to do anything. I felt ashamed. I also felt, I was a Supreme once, *a Supreme* on ADC!

"Sometimes when I cashed an ADC food order at the store, people would mention it," Flo said. "Sometimes people would put their heads down like they felt sorry for me. And that made me feel even worse. . . . I didn't want anyone to feel sorry for me. For a long, long time I just dreaded cashing those checks; I just hated it. . . . I felt like a nobody. I almost forgot who I was or what I had been."

At this time in her life, Flo said, "I couldn't stand to hear music. It upset me because I was there at one time, and wasn't singing anymore. . . . Whenever I heard music, I would get anxious and nervous. I would just get a funny feeling inside. Especially if I heard a Supremes tune that I sang on, I would just get humble inside, like bottles dropping off. I couldn't stand to hear a song by the Supremes; I just couldn't. So I just didn't play any records or the radio, just the TV."

One day, even television betrayed Flo. She suddenly realized she was watching a film clip of the Supremes, with Cindy Birdsong in her place, performing on *The Ed Sullivan Show*. "I just turned the TV off. I couldn't stand to watch it." After that, she said, "Whenever they came on TV I would turn it off, or if they played anywhere in Detroit, I wouldn't go and see it. I just couldn't stand it."

Soon she found herself drinking more frequently than before. Her drink of choice was beer. Drinking more often "was bad because I was drinking under pressure," she said. "I was depressed. If I'm happy and I drink beer, that's fine. If I'm depressed and I drink beer, it gets all distorted. Just one can, and it seems like I'm drunk. And I found out that that's no cure for any kind of heartache."

In this state, Florence soon began to express frustration with what she saw as Patmon, Young's ineffectual work on her behalf. "I would call Patmon's office, and they would say 'he's not in'; so I would ask to speak to Attorney Tate, and they'd say 'he's not in.' Anybody I asked to speak to, nobody was in."

She added, "There were a lot of questions in my mind, but I couldn't get any answers. I had hired Patmon, Young, and Kirk to get this information and to sue Berry Gordy, but it seemed like Patmon, Young, and Kirk was in a way affiliated with Motown, and I didn't know this."

In fact Patmon, Young had no connection with Motown. Florence was apparently confused by the firm's handling of Holland-Dozier-Holland's suit against Motown in 1968. After H-D-H had left the company and Gordy sued them for breach of contract, Patmon, Young had been the firm that counter-sued Motown on behalf of H-D-H. In 1972 both suits were settled out of court.

Given her despair and frustration, it's lucky Flo wasn't listening to the radio around this time. The last Supremes hit in which she had sung was being played night and day. It was titled, ironically, "Reflections" and included the line "Reflections of the way life used to be."

In an ideal world, Flo might have been able to pull herself out of her downward spiral. She certainly had a large, supportive family and many friends who might have helped her. But her heart was broken.

21

Inside the Mental Ward

You're not an alcoholic; you're just under a lot of pressure and strain.

—One of Flo's doctors, in response
to her request for treatment for
alcoholism

A RAY OF HOPE pierced Flo's deep depression when the *Detroit Free Press*, on January 17, 1975, printed the story "Ex-Supreme Broke, on ADC," which told a mass audience what Florence and some of her relatives already knew too well. The story began

Not so long ago, Florence Ballard Chapman was the toast of three continents as one of the original Supremes.

Now she says most of her neighbors don't know who she is.

Not so long ago, Florence Ballard Chapman drove a plum rose El Dorado, then graduated to a golden Fleetwood.

Now she walks, she says, but only a few steps at a time, because she broke her ankle last month.

Not so long ago, Florence Ballard Chapman was an expectant young mother. She lived in a substantial house on Buena Vista and she thought she had enough money to last the rest of her life.

Now, she says, she's broke. Her old house, which she says was taken from her by foreclosure, is boarded up. She and her husband are separated. She receives payments as aid to dependent children.

The day the story appeared, "my phone was just flying off the hook, and my stomach was crawling," Flo said. "Every time the phone would ring, I would get nervous. There was so much excitement, and I wasn't used to it. I'd been out of it for so many years, away from reporters and publicity. . . . It lasted for weeks. A lot of reporters were calling, from California, New York, from everywhere, from all over; a lot of them were saying they were sorry for what had happened—they didn't know. A lot of people said they thought I was wealthy—I had lots of money and I was doing great. Then some people here in Detroit called and were saying, 'We didn't even know you still lived in Detroit.' The majority of the people who called me said it was a shame, that I got a rotten deal, that Berry Gordy was really wrong for what he did to me, and that they just didn't know my predicament, and that they were sorry. I did not get one bad phone call. I am well liked, always was."

One caller in the first frantic days after the story was published offered Flo a job in a nursery school. She avoided returning his call for a week, and when she finally did, he told her that the job had already been filled.

"He acted like he was kind of mad, like 'You know, you're on ADC, but you mustn't be too concerned about getting off it 'cause you didn't call.' So I said, 'Hmm, well, sorry.' He'd wanted to pay me something like eighty dollars every two weeks, but I don't know if it was full-time work or not. And I said, 'Hmm, I'm getting a little bit more than that in my check.'"

Another reader "called me from the Riverboat Club in New York and said I could sing in his club for five hundred dollars for three weeks, but I'd have to pay my own expenses." Aware of the cost of hotels in New York City, Flo said "Uh-uh."

Tantalizingly, Jack Ashford, a former Motown musician who was working with former Motown executive Barney Ales at Ales's new record company, asked Flo if she wanted to record. For some reason it didn't come to anything. "We were supposed to get together to hear some tunes that he had written," Flo said, "but we never did."

In June, Michigan congressman John Conyers's office called Flo one morning, inquiring if she would sing at a Joanne Little benefit concert scheduled for later that month in Detroit's Ford Auditorium. Little, a black prison inmate, had been accused of killing a corrections officer she said had raped her. She was on trial in North Carolina.

"I said, 'No, I'm sick,'" Flo said, "but then I thought, 'I'm tired of saying I'm sick.' I called back and said 'I'll do it.' The song they wanted me to sing was 'I Am Woman,' a Helen Reddy song, so I got the record and learned the tune."

Flo said she was worried—"I didn't even know if I could sing; I didn't even know if I had a voice or not. I couldn't hear myself, and I was scared to death—wow, was I scared—because I hadn't been up onstage for so long." She was even afraid she would forget the words of the song. An onlooker described her as "very quiet" before her performance, an uncharacteristic moment for the formerly talkative Supreme.

The Deadly Nightshade, Flo's assigned backup group, greeted her with wild enthusiasm. The group idolized the Supremes. Some wires must have been crossed, however, because the Deadly Nightshade was not familiar with "I Am Woman." But the group, realizing the consequences for Flo's morale if her first public appearance in years was a failure, held a practice session backstage and learned the tune.

Despite her worries, Flo performed well in front of a packed house, which included Gloria Steinem and fellow Detroiter Lily Tomlin. "The people were so warm," she said. "They were so great; they stood up like they were just so happy to see me up there, and then I began to relax." She was rewarded with a standing ovation.

Pamela Brandt of the Deadly Nightshade continues the story in Gillian G. Gaar's book *She's a Rebel: The History of Women in Rock 'n' Roll*:

The crowd really, really loved her. It was obvious that she was who they were waiting for. Then she walked off the stage and was standing on the side, and it was obvious that she wanted to come back on, but she was real insecure. So I ran over and said, "Come on, you have to come back! They're dying for you!" and grabbed her hand and started dragging her back. As soon as she got one foot on the stage the audience erupted anew. She was bowing, and then she straightened her shoulders, got completely secure again, and strutted across the stage in front of us. And as she passed us, she threw back her head and whispered, "By any chance, would you happen to know 'Come See About Me?'" We said, "Yes, yes, yes, yes!" She sang lead, and we got to do her old parts and Mary Wilson's parts. She was fantastic!

The crowd gave Flo her second standing ovation of the day. It was the last ovation Flo Ballard would ever receive for a performance.

At Mary Wilson's instigation, Flo also appeared in August 1975 at a Magic Mountain, California, performance of the third generation of Supremes, consisting of Mary Wilson, Cindy Birdsong, and Scherrie Payne. In 1974, Payne had replaced Jean Terrell, who had replaced Diana Ross. Although Flo didn't sing, tears appeared in her eyes as she heard the audience applaud, and yell, "Flo, we love you."

According to Flo, after that concert she refused an offer made via Mary to return to Motown. In her words, "Everything was laid out. They were going to have me do vocal training and everything, but they weren't going to put me back into the Supremes. Who would want to go back after you'd been stepped on like that? No, not me, no. I'd rather just live in Detroit and be poor for the rest of my life than to go back to Motown."

According to Mary Wilson's version, all that Wilson did was encourage Flo to find a good producer, get some good songs written, and get her career going again. Wilson said Flo told her she was just no longer capable of doing it.

Flo's downslide continued when she returned to Detroit. Flo said later that the *Free Press* story and the resulting avalanche of national and international publicity had primed her to expect the suits she had filed to end quickly in her favor. "I thought [something] would happen overnight," Flo said. When it didn't, the end result was deeper disappointment.

Finally the phone stopped ringing, and Flo's depression deepened. The relapse took her to new psychological lows. She was readmitted to Henry Ford Hospital's psychiatric unit in the fall of 1975, and this time she stayed there for two weeks. "I had to go somewhere because I knew that I was just falling completely apart. . . . I even began to hate myself—I really did—I hated myself so much because I drank beer, because I didn't have any money, because I couldn't do anything for my kids, because I was on ADC. It just seemed like everything was falling in on me, and I just couldn't take it. I didn't want to go back in the hospital or anywhere else and leave my kids. That was very hard to do, to leave the children, but I just had to do something. I mean, I just couldn't see myself going on and on and on like this.

"When I went to the hospital again, the doctor said the same thing he said the first time I went in there: that I just needed a rest to clear my mind. They had me on two milligrams of Librium, nothing strong. And after that nothing.

"A young doctor came in the morning after I had admitted myself, and I told him I'd like to see a psychiatrist. He said to me, 'Do you see anything crawling on the walls? Do you see any rats? Do you feel like climbing the walls?' I looked at him, and I said, 'What!?' and started laughing. Then he said, 'What do you want to see a psychiatrist for?'"

This question, and Flo's answer, could have prompted a turning point in Flo's life. Now in her second stay in what amounted to a mental institution, Flo was digging down deep into herself to unearth what very likely was by now her major problem: "I'm an alcoholic," she told the doctor. "I can't understand why I keep drinking and why I keep feeling so bad all the time." Here Flo had frankly and voluntarily announced her problem to an allegedly qualified medical professional; but instead of telling Flo that she may have felt bad because alcohol is a depressant and that drinking can lead to misguided actions that cause further depression, the doctor replied breezily, "It's easy. You lost everything you had," according to Flo. He then asked her, "How much beer do you drink?" She said, "Maybe eight cans twice a week or something."

The "or something" was significant. Like most people with an alcohol problem, Flo probably drank more than embarrassment allowed her to admit. But the doctor continued to back away from his patient's problem. In response to her admission that she drank a minimum of sixteen cans of beer a week, he said, "That's nothing. I drink maybe a six-pack a day."

Flo pressed the issue. She told the doctor, "I've got to be an alcoholic," and asked that she be allowed to go to what she called "sessions for alcoholics," possibly Alcoholics Anonymous meetings, that were held at the hospital. The doctor continued to resist. "You don't need to go to those," he insisted. "Yes I do; yes I do," Flo said. Finally, he relented. "Well, it won't hurt," he said but added, "If you want to go you can go, but you're not an alcoholic; you're just under a lot of pressure and strain."

The first meeting made an impression on Flo. "I saw people there that had liver damage, that couldn't walk to the classes, that had to be pushed to the classes in wheelchairs. It was pitiful," she said. "One lady had her whole ankle wrapped up; her feet were infected from drinking, from her liver; and her face, her pores were just wide open—her skin was, like, gone. Everybody told how much they drink in these classes. One guy said he spent $169 on whiskey a week. I listened, and I thought, 'That's unbelievable! He couldn't! He couldn't!' I said, 'How could you drink that much? That's a lot of booze.' He said he was drinking three or four fifths a day. Unbelievable. I said, 'I drink maybe six or eight cans of beer maybe twice a week.' One of the ladies in the class looked at me and said, 'You don't have any business here. Hell, beer ain't nothing! Look at me, I drink fifths a day!' I thought, 'Wow! Should I leave or stay?'"

Flo said she kept going to the meetings while she was hospitalized. "It was interesting to learn how alcohol affects different parts of your body, your stomach, your intestines, your bladder, your liver," she said. "And all of it just made me shake. They were telling the class how the liver just expands and expands and becomes so big because it's sore from alcohol—ugh. After that I said, 'Wow!' but I stayed in there. I just hung on in there and got as much out of it as I could."

If Flo had been encouraged just a little more, she might have kept going to meetings after leaving the hospital. She didn't. But even with her short exposure to what was probably AA, she managed to take some lessons home with her.

"Some of the things they said made a lot of sense," she noted. "Like 'Live for one day and don't worry about tomorrow, because tomorrow is not promised,' and it's not. And when I came out, I just told everybody, 'Hey, look what alcohol's doing to you.'"

Flo had also begun reading the Bible frequently during her second hospitalization. She said she did so "because I was saying to myself, 'Who can I trust? Everybody I turn to just takes things, or takes money.'

"Finally I began to just accept that I was on ADC and that I was going to remain like that for the rest of my life, that nothing would be done about my rights or lawsuits or anything, that my rights were all just violated, and who gave a damn. . . . So I just said, well, forget it. I just put it out of my mind."

Florence had stopped going to church in her teens, when her singing career began, but "my mind stayed on God even when I was with the Supremes," she said. Flo stuck with her Bible reading after leaving the hospital because "it seems like it's always something in the Bible to put me at ease." The book, and particularly the Psalms, taught her to "trust in God, not in man."

Once, while Flo was living in her final residence, her mother and one of her daughters were sick, and she had to take both of them to the doctor, then watch over them after she brought them back home. "That night" she said, "I couldn't rest. I would fall asleep and wake up, fall asleep and wake up. So finally I went to sleep and woke back up at 6:00 A.M. I began to wash clothes and do a whole bunch of housework. And that still wouldn't help. So finally I said, "God, I can't even sleep; I can't rest—I'm restless.

"I opened the book and began to read Psalms, and it said there, 'You will sleep, and you will awake in peace.' I fell soundly asleep that night. Next morning I woke up feeling terrific, really great."

Flo also started listening to music again. "I turn it up and I play the radio all day, play it in the car, everywhere. And it doesn't bother me now," she said in 1975. "When a Supremes record is played, I just listen and say, 'It sounds great.' Because, I guess, I've faced reality. I say to myself a lot also, 'The past is just dead.' I'm no longer trying to find a way of escaping from reality. I never will, not anymore. Or drink to make myself happy. Or do anything to make myself happy, for that matter. If there's something that's causing you pain, then instead of you drinking or taking tranquilizers or anything to get rid of the pain, you should just live through the pain, cry, scream, holler, do anything to get it out of you. I had been holding it all in me.

"By drinking, you can forget; you can feel happy or sad. In my case, it just made me sadder. When you take tranquilizers, they relax you; you go to sleep. But when you wake up, it's another day. . . . And after you stop taking them, your thoughts are still there. Your thoughts are actually still there anyway while you're taking them, but they're not as severe. And if anything makes me unhappy or if I become depressed right now, then I'm just depressed; I have to just face it. And in a few days it will pass. I've learned now how it goes away."

Flo also said that the publicity about her plight had helped her mentally, even if it hadn't done much for her financially. "It was out. Everybody knew that Motown had definitely taken some money, and so had this attorney, Leonard Baun." Some small part of Florence may have been looking forward to June, when a court hearing on Patmon, Young's suit against Baun was scheduled. But the case was postponed until August. "I got mad, and they said, 'We don't think you're well enough,' that I wasn't strong enough mentally," she said.

"But we were all really cramped. Me and the three children were sleeping in one bedroom, in twin beds. I got very depressed. I wanted to move away from there so my children could stretch out." For that, she needed more than her welfare check.

Luckily for Flo, a settlement of her case against Baun was in the works. "Baun's lawyers were calling Patmon," Flo said, "and asking them, 'How much money does she want?'" Patmon, trying to raise the ante, was refusing to even talk to Baun's lawyers. Flo misinterpreted this, concluding that "evidently Patmon didn't give a damn about nothing." According to Flo's account, she and her brother Billy actually went around their own counsel and negotiated directly with Leonard Baun's lawyers, accepting what Patmon, Young considered a lowball offer.

Patmon, Young were evidently irritated with the settlement offer Flo accepted, which was $82,000, of which $20,000 would go to Patmon, Young for their work on her behalf. "They claimed they were working really hard, and that if I hadn't settled, I could have gotten way much more money," Flo noted.

Harry Okrent, Baun's law partner, then offered Flo $10,000 to settle with him. Okrent had said that he never represented Flo and that he had nothing to do with Baun's treatment of her. Flo said that Patmon told her, "If Okrent can give you the $10,000, then he can give you $25,000." But Flo said, "I looked at Okrent. He was so old; he looked so sickly. I said, 'God, maybe I don't even want the $10,000!'" and refused Patmon's advice. She took the $10,000.

In the *Dreamgirls* movie, the Florence Ballard character comments, "I blew half a million in two years," after she left Motown. In reality, Baun had walked away with most of Flo's Motown settlement money, and the settlements with Baun and Okrent netted her a grand total of $72,000, a far cry from what she was due, particularly had she received royalties.

Although the Lost Supreme had once again come out on the short end of the financial stick, the settlement money did cheer her and improve her situation, enabling her to buy a car and move to a house big enough for herself, her husband, and her children. Maybe things were looking up.

22

To Err Is Human

> *How could we have grown up together and then turn out to be not liking each other? I think we all have problems.*
>
> —Florence Ballard

FLO'S SITUATION HAD improved, but she had fallen into a pattern. An injustice would be committed against her. She would respond with everything she had, putting her foes on the defensive. Unhinged, they would stagger backward, giving her an opportunity to follow through. She would then give up her opportunity, drop her guard, and allow herself to be cheated or pushed aside. She followed this pattern with Diana Ross; Leonard Baun; Harry Okrent; Tommy Chapman; the men who kidnapped, robbed, and may have planned to kill her; and many other people and entities, including Motown.

Florence always characterized her tendency to let her opponents off easy as a combination of disgust, sorrow for her foe, and fatigue. Of accepting the settlement from Baun, she said she did so because she thought, "Well, this can go on forever and ever and ever. And they said Leonard Baun is $100,000 in debt to the Internal Revenue. The guy's messed up, getting ready to get disbarred and everything. . . . So I just went on and took his insurance money and invested it and said, 'Well, let's see what happens with that.'"

Flo said she did not protest when Patmon, Young received their $20,000 fee for bringing about the settlement, even though she mistakenly believed they were working for Motown, her archenemy. "Patmon, Young, and Kirk should have received nothing, as far as I'm concerned," Flo said. "But I just said, 'Take it; the hell with it,' because I was just tired of the same thing over and over and over again. . . . I should have kept the $20,000 I let Patmon and them get; I should have kept it and sued them—that's what I should have done—but I was tired of it, and I said, 'I'm just sick of it' . . . so I said, 'the hell with it.'"

As for her feelings toward Diana Ross and Mary Wilson, Flo expressed ambivalence in 1975. After she and Ross had both left the Supremes, she said, "Diane would come to town, and she wouldn't even call to say hello or anything," Flo said. "I thought it was kind of ridiculous, all three of us growing up together, then turning out to dislike each other so. I didn't dislike her, because I said to myself if Diane had been in the predicament I was in, I would be right there to help her. And to this day, if she ever should fall into a bad predicament, I would still help her as much as I could. But I guess she felt different."

She excused Ross's refusals to mingle with fans, which were widely criticized, on the basis of exhaustion. While noting that Diane "has an ego, a big ego, a very big ego," Flo added, "Diane always liked her privacy. I think we all do. People, the fans, don't understand how artists feel. Diane possibly could have been very tired, so she just didn't want to be bothered. And the fans will take it the wrong way.

"A lot of fans have come to me and said, 'Diane is very nasty. She has a very nasty personality,'" Flo said. "And I would say, 'Well, she's just tired.' And taking on all those leads, she had to be just worn out, because she had a lot of sleepless nights that she couldn't rest, insomnia and this and that. She had quite a few problems."

Flo did finally manage to reach Diana by telephone in 1975, a difficult task considering the vigilance of Diana's staff. "She's back to the Diane I knew when we were growing up," she said. "I think the reason basically of her changing is because she's now more relaxed; she's not under so much of the strain of performing every night as before.

"We had a very long, very nice woman-to-woman talk," Flo said. "She seemed more relaxed, more earthy. She's making movies, and I had to give her credit. I went to see that one movie, *Lady Sings the Blues*, and I must say, I cried—I did! I guess because we grew up together, the three of us were so much like sisters. That scene in *Lady Sings the Blues* where people are throwing stuff through the windows of the bus took me back to Macon, Georgia, and I said, 'Wow!' She really did a fantastic acting job in that film. I give her all the credit in the world. I used to say to myself, 'How could we have grown up together and then turn out to be not liking each other?' I think we all have problems."

In praising Ross, Flo even compared her assertiveness favorably with what she perceived as Mary Wilson's passivity, saying, "As far as I'm concerned, I would rather deal with Diane than I would with, say, Mary. Because Diane is more of a straightforward person, she doesn't bite her tongue, she will tell you how she feels, and she'll tell anybody else how she feels." However, Flo went on to praise Mary, noting, "Mary always kept in touch, Mary never forgot the kids around Christmas, she would always give them whatever she could, and Mary didn't have that much."

Flo not only got back in touch with Diana that year but also reacquainted herself with the glorious recordings that she, Diana, and Mary had made during their heyday.

"I didn't realize how many albums we recorded until lately," she said in 1975, "because I had forgotten about all of the albums—there were so many. We were always recording, recording, recording. Then I heard some tune on the radio not too long ago and I said, 'God—phew!—I forgot all about that one.'" When Flo heard one of those old tunes, she said, she turned the radio up. "It sounds good to me," she said, "and the memories . . . and then I say to myself, 'Boy, that record sold a lot of copies, and nearly every one they play was a million-seller.'

"Sometimes I have regrets and wish I was back in the group, but a lot of times I say to myself, 'Would it be worth it to go back into it and have the same thing happen again?' Because basically, Mary Wilson, the only original Supreme now—she's still singing, but she didn't get what she deserved either, moneywise."

23

The Lost Supreme

*When we reached the cemetery, it was just Flo's
family, the pallbearers, The Four Tops, and me.*

—Mary Wilson, *Dreamgirl: My Life as
a Supreme*

ON A WINTER DAY in 1976, Flo visited her mother's house, where her sister
Linda was also living, and ate one ice cube after another right out of the freezer.
When her mother asked her why, Flo said, "I feel hot all the time." Then she
told Mrs. Ballard, "If anything happens to me, Mommy, take my kids."

Flo returned home without incident, but her condition worsened during
the night. Her daughter Nicole called Linda the next morning to tell her that
something was seriously wrong.

Linda was anxious to reach her sister but couldn't start her car until late
morning. Nicole, growing increasingly frantic, also kept trying to reach her
father, who was working as a chauffeur for a local minister. She finally contacted Chapman by phone a little after noon. Linda was also calling him. "After
I kept pleading with him to do something," Linda said, "he finally picked me
up." Linda later criticized Chapman for not coming home immediately.
"Tommy acted as if Flo being sick was interfering with his schedule," she said.

When Linda and Tommy reached Flo's house, Linda found her sister, who
had protected her from a rock-throwing boy approximately a quarter of a cen-

tury before, lying on the floor, unable to move. "I had to use all my strength to pick her up off the floor and put her on the couch," Linda said. "Tommy didn't help me. When I asked her what was wrong, she told me, in a robotic voice, that she couldn't move from the waist down."

"If anything happens to me," Flo said again, "Take care of my baby," apparently referring to Lisa, her youngest daughter.

Linda, who died in 2007, described Tommy's attitude toward the seriously ill Flo as "nonchalant." She told Flo that she was going to be all right and called an ambulance to take the former Supreme to Mt. Carmel Mercy Hospital. Linda stayed with the children while Tommy went with Flo to the hospital, where doctors discovered she had a blood clot in a coronary artery.

Tommy said later that by 2:30 A.M. the doctors had told him they felt that Flo was "pulling through" and he could go home.

"Before I left the hospital, she was smiling and had just fallen off to sleep," Chapman said. "About 7:30 A.M., I received a call from the hospital asking me to get there as soon as possible. When I got there, I waited for about thirty minutes, and then the doctor came out and told me my wife was dead."

Flo died on February 22, 1976. The cause on the death certificate was coronary artery thrombosis. She was thirty-two.

It was eight years to the day after Flo had signed the final agreement giving up her membership in the Supremes. This may not have been a coincidence. Studies have shown that even gravely ill people often hang on to life in order to die on a day that is meaningful to them.

The Wayne County medical examiner, Dr. Werner Spitz, indicated in news articles at the time that he'd been told that before Flo had been admitted to the emergency room, she had been drinking and taking two different medications, one to facilitate weight loss and the other to counteract high blood pressure.

The autopsy told a different story. According to assistant medical examiner James Mullaney, the physician who performed the procedure, there were no drugs in Flo's system except a small amount of Seniquan, an antidepressant.

Although Dr. Mullaney indicated he'd been told that Flo also had been taking Tenuate, an appetite suppressant, and Lasix, a drug used to treat excessive fluid accumulation and swelling, he discovered no traces of these drugs in her system and only "a trace" of alcohol.

What killed Flo, according to the autopsy, was a combination of heart disease, a blood clot, hypertension, and "obesity." Elsewhere in the report, however, Dr. Mullaney described Flo as "somewhat obese," and that was probably the right way to put it. A person of her height and weight—the autopsy states that the five foot seven Flow weighed 195 pounds at the time of her death—is certainly heavy but not morbidly obese.

I attended Flo's funeral, which was held at the New Bethel Baptist Church. The congregation was ministered to by the Reverend C. L. Franklin, father of Aretha Franklin. Before the funeral began, a group of about five thousand fans wearing everything from evening gowns to work clothes had gathered outside the church. When a limousine pulled up next to the church steps and Diana Ross jumped out, the fans booed. Diana's mother, standing nearby, looked extremely unhappy.

It's not clear if Diana had been invited. Tommy Chapman, Flo's husband, had made the funeral arrangements, and he died in the 1980s. But Flo's daughters and other relatives said that invitation or no invitation, Diana knew the family would welcome her. Inside the church, Diana marched down the center aisle and was seated next to Tommy in the front pew reserved for Flo's family members. Taking Flo's youngest girl, Lisa, from her father, Diana placed the child in her lap. The picture of the former "first Supreme" holding the little daughter of the deceased "lost Supreme" would be printed in newspapers across the country and around the world. It was the only image of the funeral most people saw, making the occasion an emblem of Diana's starhood rather than a celebration of Florence's life and a scene of mourning for her death.

Every act from Motown sent a floral arrangement. Diana's said, "I Love You, Blondie." Berry Gordy's said, "Good Bye, Flo."

Just after Reverend Franklin completed the funeral ceremony, Diana jumped up and said, "Can I have the microphone please? Mary and I would like to have a silent prayer."

According to Wilson, Diana had not told her she was planning to do this. The two weren't even on speaking terms. But Mary could hardly refuse to stand up beside Diana at her friend's funeral. "I believe nothing disappears, and Flo will always be with us," Diana said. When she handed the mike to Mary, all Mary could think of to say was "I loved her very much."

As the mourners filed out of the church, the organist played "Someday We'll Be Together"—a Supremes hit recorded and performed after Flo had been thrown out of the group—again and again. The crowd pushed toward Flo's coffin, and the pallbearers—Duke Fakir, Obie Benson, Levi Stubbs, Lawrence Payton, Marv Johnson, and Thearon Hill—had to be escorted by attendants. The onlookers pressed forward with such energy that the attendants tried to slow them down by throwing into their midst the flower arrangements that had been sent by Flo's competitors and employers. The crowd destroyed the arrangements.

"It was pandemonium," Linda said. "The fans started jumping on top of the hearse, taking Flo's flowers, trying to get something that belonged to her." When the burial party reached the cemetery, Detroit Memorial Park, only Flo's family, the pallbearers, the Four Tops, and Mary Wilson were there.

Flo's body was buried under a gravestone that read simply. "Florence Glenda Chapman, Beloved Wife and Mother, June 30, 1943–Feb. 22, 1976." The only indication on the gravestone that she had had a musical career was a carving of two musical notes between the dates of her birth and death.

Flo's mother, Lurlee, was understandably absent at the burial. She had already lost five children at various stages of their lives. "I can't stand to see another child buried," Mrs. Ballard had told her family.

Also absent from the cemetery, however, was Diana. The only person other than Mary who had shared Flo's greatest moments had skipped out on Flo's final performance.

24
Flo Sums It Up

My friends said, 'Here comes Flo; close the doors.'

—Florence Ballard

FLORENCE BALLARD'S talent propelled her from a world of poverty and insignificance into one of luxury and fame. Then she was cruelly tossed back. In her last words to the author, shortly before her death, she summed up how that felt:

> My friends said, "Here comes Flo; close the doors." I wanted to forget who Florence Ballard was. All I wanted to do was live for my children.
>
> My friends couldn't understand that I was fighting something. "Help me get back on my feet so I won't fall again," I said, but my friends didn't hear me. . . .
>
> I'm not suffering. I'm not crying. I'm just tired. Everything I try goes the wrong way. . . .
>
> I used to dream that if I won a lawsuit, I would have minks and diamonds. But when I got some money, all I tried to do was fill the house with happiness. If the kids could be happy, the money would be well spent. . . .
>
> I can't find myself in singing. Lord knows I tried. Everybody says I'm a big star, but everywhere I go, I'm stopped in my tracks. Where do you go when you're a big star?

171

25

Where's the Rest of Me?

I had done it. I had won the poker hand.

—Berry Gordy, in his 1994
autobiography, *To Be Loved: The
Music, the Magic, the Memories of
Motown*

THE SUPREMES OFFICIALLY disbanded in 1977, although groups using that name, including "tribute" groups, are still performing. In 1983 a television special celebrating Motown's twenty-fifth anniversary brought Diana Ross, Mary Wilson, and Cindy Birdsong onstage for a very brief reunion of the almost-original Supremes. Wilson recalled that during their performance of "Someday We'll Be Together," when Wilson and Birdsong kept pace with Ross as she advanced onstage toward the audience, Ross turned and showed Wilson toward the back of the stage. A few seconds later, when Wilson tried to use the mike, Ross forced her hand down so she couldn't use it. Motown edited this embarrassing footage from the televised show.

In 2000, twenty-four years after Flo's death, Diana Ross organized a "Return to Love" tour of the Supremes, inviting the only other living original Supreme, Mary Wilson, as well as Cindy Birdsong, to join her on the tour. Although Ross's take from the concert would have been an estimated $15 to $20 million, she bridled when Wilson refused a $3 million offer. (Birdsong indicated that she would have been happy with the $1 million she was offered.) Wilson had asked for a modest $4 million and also suggested the top ticket price be lowered from $250 a ticket so that more people could afford to see the show. Ross then cut off negotiations with Wilson and Birdsong and signed up two other ex-Supremes, Scherrie Payne and Lynda Laurence, for the tour. Predictably, the tour's Detroit venue was half empty, and the Detroit performance became the last of the tour.

Mary Wilson, sixty-five as of the printing of this book, lives in Las Vegas and is still performing solo. After Diana Ross left the Supremes in 1970, Wilson doggedly kept the group going through numerous personnel changes until it finally disbanded seven years later. She followed up her bestselling 1986 book, *Dreamgirl: My Life as a Supreme* with *Supreme Faith: Someday We'll Be Together* in 1990. She has also worked in musicals and in off-Broadway plays.

After leaving the Supremes, Diana Ross, also sixty-five as of the printing of this book, went on to become a major single act, superstar, and diva and in 1981 left Motown entirely. The *Guinness Book of World Records* has since proclaimed her the most successful female singer of all time. She is still performing solo. Although she lived in Greenwich, Connecticut, for years, in late 2006 she moved to Los Angeles.

As for the musical legacy of the third original Supreme, some small progress was made over many years to resuscitate Florence Ballard's music and reputation. After her fans crusaded for the release of the songs Flo had recorded for ABC but that remained unheard, Spectrum Music of England, a company owned by Universal Music, which had absorbed Motown, finally put out the album in 2001 as a CD titled *The Supreme Florence Ballard*. It includes fourteen songs Flo recorded as a solo artist for ABC: "Like You Babe," "Yesterday," "Yours Until Tomorrow," "It's Not Unusual," "The Impossible Dream," "It Doesn't Matter How I Say It (It's What I Say That Matters)," "Stay in Love," "Walk on By," "Goin' out of My Head," "You Bring out the Sweetness in Me," "Everything Wonderful," "Love Ain't Love," "Forever Faithful," and "My Heart." Also included are four Supremes songs in which Flo was featured as the lead: "Buttered Popcorn," "Ain't That Good News," "Hey Baby," and "Heavenly Father."

Berry Gordy, now seventy-nine, sold Motown to MCA Incorporated in 1988 for $61 million. He exulted in this, writing in his autobiography, "from eight hundred dollars to $61 million, I had done it. I had won the poker hand." He now lives in Los Angeles, where he is working on a twelve-part television series about Motown due for release in September 2009.

The attorney who walked away with the bulk of Flo's Motown settlement money, Leonard Baun, died in 1983, at age sixty. After his death, the Michigan State Bar destroyed the records of the disbarment proceedings against him, a favor they perform for all deceased members of the Bar.

Flo's husband, Tommy Chapman, survived his wife by nine years. After her death in 1976, even though Chapman was living in Detroit, his three daughters were taken in by Flo's sister Linda. In 1982, according to Linda, when Flo's mother, Lurlee, lay on her deathbed, she called Linda in and told her the kids should go to Tommy. Then she apparently reconsidered. She called Linda back in and told her Linda should keep the kids "because he [Tommy] just can't do it."

In a 1984 newspaper article about Chapman in the *Daily Reveille*, published in Baton Rouge, Louisiana, where Chapman was working as a bus driver, he boasted about his experience as a manager of musical acts. "I was in the music business long before Motown even thought about it," he asserted.

In fact, he attempted to get back into that business after Flo's death. His longtime lady friend in Baton Rouge, Florence Lollis, one of Chapman's fellow bus drivers, said that Chapman had organized a blues band there called "Flo and the Young and the Restless," with Flo Lollis as the vocalist, in an attempt to restart his musical career. Lollis said, however, that she wasn't enthusiastic about a musical career and had participated in the band just "to make him happy."

Friends of Chapman said he came home from work one night, said he didn't feel well, and went into the bedroom to take a nap. He then died in his sleep. According to the records of the bus company that employed Chapman, he died of a heart attack on May 11, 1985, while off-duty and is buried in Baton Rouge. He was forty-five at the time of his death.

Lollis said Chapman was preoccupied during the last years of his life by the end of his wife's career and her death, the poverty in which he felt his three daughters were living, and the wrongs he felt Motown had perpetrated on his wife and on himself. Chapman "really wanted to hold on to the past," she said. One of the reasons they broke up, a few months before his death, she said, was the stress he suffered from his memories of the past and the need he felt to keep sending money to his children, who he believed should have received more money from Motown.

Most of Florence Ballard's family remains in Detroit, including her three daughters. Michelle Chapman lives in a small Detroit house adorned with portraits of her mother. Her twin sister, Nicole Chapman, strongly resembles her mother and speaks of her fondly. Flo's youngest daughter, Lisa Chapman, was almost overcome by grief while appearing on behalf of her late mother when the Supremes were inducted into the Rock and Roll Hall of Fame in 1988.

All three of Florence Ballard's children are on welfare.

Afterword

The *Dreamgirls* Resurrections

And I am telling you I'm not going.

—Effie Melody White

FLORENCE BALLARD has been resurrected twice: once by the Broadway musical *Dreamgirls*, which opened in 1981, and more recently by the *Dreamgirls* movie, which premiered in late 2006. Both represent the Flo Ballard story as millions of people probably wish it had happened.

The *Dreamgirls* movie is about the rise of an all-female singing group, the "Dreamettes"—later the "Dreams" (read "Primettes"/"Supremes")—in Detroit during the 1960s. Actress Jennifer Hudson, playing Effie Melody White, the Flo Ballard character, won the Best Supporting Actress Oscar for her portrayal of the Lost Supreme. The group is managed by a former car salesman named Curtis. (The Supremes were managed by a former auto worker named Berry.) Curtis replaces lead singer Effie with Deena (Diana) in order to attract a white as well as black audience for the group. So far, pretty close.

Unreality enters when Effie becomes pregnant with Curtis's child. The movie pole-vaults into another, even more fictional universe when Deena resists Curtis's offer to be group lead, saying she can't sing as well as Effie.

The climax of the movie occurs with the number "And I Am Telling You I'm Not Going," which is about Effie's expulsion from the Dreams. During that number, Effie is confronted by her brother, Clarence Conrad, also known as C.C. (just as Flo was confronted by her brother Cornell earlier in her life, after she had dropped out of school). Fiction returns for the finale when Effie's solo career starts slowly but then, with an assist from Deena, seems to take off.

(Fans have surely realized that in almost every case, the musical and film character's name starts with the same letter as the real person's name, or with the letter before it in the alphabet, or sounds almost exactly like it, as in the substitution of the fictional "Jolly Jenkins" for the real Cholly Atkins.)

Mary Wilson was a fan of the *Dreamgirls* musical and movie. Diana Ross said in early 2007 that she never saw the theatrical production and joked that if she saw the movie, she'd do so with her lawyers. Apparently she did not realize how gently the movie treated her.

That the Ballard/Supremes/Motown story, which took place in the 1960s and '70s, has resulted in numerous newspaper, magazine, and television stories, fiction and nonfiction books, a Broadway musical, and a movie is an obvious tribute to the story's staying power. It's also a testimonial to the story's roots in the dark side of the American Dream, the unfairness of the recording industry, the fight against that unfairness, and the attempt to meld black and white Americans into one people.

Although the original Supremes stopped singing together in 1967, the multiple retelling of their story since then continues to add to their status as icons. The Supremes' own performances, the performances of the actors playing them in both *Dreamgirls* productions, and the performances of many other stage and screen actors whose appearance and presence refers to the Supremes have made the image of three glamorous black women—Florence Ballard, Diana Ross, and Mary Wilson—cooing into a microphone almost as much a symbol of American culture as Coca-Cola.

Imitators continue to use this iconic power to attract the unwary. According to a 2006 *Detroit News* blog:

> They're coming . . . three women billing themselves as "The Supremes," playing a special "Christmas" show on Dec. 1 at the Ford Community & Per-

forming Arts Center. . . . But don't get too excited, Diana and Mary haven't kissed and made up. . . . Close up that wallet. . . . This group, fronted by '70–'80s "Supreme" Kaaren Ragland, didn't record for Motown Records.

This group didn't, but the original Supremes—Florence Ballard, Diane Ross, and Mary Wilson—did. And if you listen, you can hear them now.

Appendix 1

Florence Ballard, Primettes, and Supremes Discography

SINGLES

The Primettes (1959–1960): Florence Ballard, Betty McGlown, Diane Ross, Mary Wilson

TITLE	LABEL	RELEASE DATE
"Tears of Sorrow" / "Pretty Baby"	Lupine 120	1960

The Primettes (1960–1961): Florence Ballard, Barbara Martin, Diane Ross, Mary Wilson

No singles

The Supremes (1961–1962): Florence Ballard, Barbara Martin, Diane Ross, Mary Wilson

TITLE	LABEL	RELEASE DATE
"I Want a Guy" / "Never Again"	Tamla 54038	03/09/1961
"Buttered Popcorn" / "Who's Loving You?"	Tamla 54045	07/21/1961

The Supremes (1962–1967): Florence Ballard, Diana Ross, Mary Wilson

TITLE	LABEL	RELEASE DATE
"Your Heart Belongs to Me" / "He's Seventeen"	Motown 1027	05/08/1962

"Let Me Go the Right Way" / "Time Changes Things"	Motown 1034	11/05/1962
"My Heart Can't Take It No More"/ "You Bring Back Memories"	Motown 1040	02/02/1963
"A Breathtaking Guy" / "Rock & Roll Banjo Band"	Motown 1044	06/12/1963
"When the Lovelight Starts Shining Through His Eyes" / "Standing at the Crossroads of Love"	Motown 1051	10/31/1963
"Run, Run, Run" / "I'm Giving You Your Freedom"	Motown 1054	02/07/1964
"Where Did Our Love Go?" (**1st #1 Hit**) / "He Means the World to Me"	Motown 1054	06/17/1964
"Baby Love" (**2nd Consecutive #1 Hit**) / "Ask Any Girl"	Motown 1066	09/17/1964
"Come See about Me" (**3rd Consecutive #1 Hit**) / Always in My Heart"	Motown 1068	10/27/1964
"Stop! In the Name of Love" (**4th Consecutive #1 Hit**) / "I'm in Love Again"	Motown 1074	02/08/1965
"Back in My Arms Again" (**5th Consecutive #1 Hit**) / "Whisper You Love Me Boy"	Motown 1075	04/15/1965
"Nothing but Heartaches" / "He Holds His Own"	Motown 1080	07/16/1965
"I Hear a Symphony" (**6th #1 Hit**) / "Who Could Ever Doubt My Love"	Motown 1083	10/06/1965
"Children's Christmas Song" / "Twinkle Twinkle Little Me"	Motown 1085	11/18/1965
"My World Is Empty without You" / "Everything's Good about You"	Motown 1089	12/29/1965
"Love Is Like an Itching in My Heart" / "He's All I Got"	Motown 1094	04/08/1966
"You Can't Hurry Love" (**7th #1 Hit**) / "Put Yourself in My Place"	Motown 1097	07/25/1966
"You Keep Me Hangin' On" (**8th #1 Hit**) / "Remove This Doubt"	Motown 1101	10/12/1966
"Love Is Here and Now You're Gone" (**9th #1 Hit**) / "There's No Stopping Us Now"	Motown 1103	01/11/1967

"The Happening" (**10th #1 Hit**) /
    "All I Know About You"   Motown 1107   03/20/1967

Diana Ross and the Supremes (1967–1970): Florence Ballard, Diana Ross, Mary Wilson (on the recorded versions of "Reflections," "Going Down for the Third Time," "I Guess I'll Always Love You," "Time Changes Things," and "Your Kiss of Fire"); **Cindy Birdsong, Diana Ross, Mary Wilson** (on all records in this period except those listed above)

Title	Label	Release Date
"Reflections" / "Going Down for the Third Time"	Motown 1111	07/24/1967
"In and Out of Love" / "I Guess I'll Always Love You"	Motown 1116	10/25/1967
"Forever Came Today" / "Time Changes Things"	Motown 1112	02/24/1968
"What the World Needs Now" / "Your Kiss of Fire"	Motown 1125	03/1968
"Some Things You Never Get Used To" / "You've Been So Wonderful to Me"	Motown 1126	05/21/1968
"Love Child" (**11th #1 Hit**) / "Will This Be the Day?"	Motown 1135	09/30/1968
"I'm Gonna Make You Love Me" / "A Place in the Sun" (with the Temptations)	Motown 1137	11/21/1968
"I'm Livin' in Shame" / "I'm So Glad I Got Somebody Like You Around"	Motown 1139	01/06/1969
"I'll Try Something New" / "The Way You Do the Things You Do" (with the Temptations)	Motown 1142	02/20/1969
"The Composer" / "The Beginning of the End"	Motown 1146	03/27/1969
"No Matter What Sign You Are" / "The Young Folks"	Motown 1148	05/09/1969
"Stubborn Kind of Fellow" / "Try It Baby" (with the Temptations)	Motown 1150	08/1969
"The Weight" / "For Better or for Worse" (with the Temptations)	Motown 1153	08/29/1969
"Someday We'll Be Together" (**12th and last #1 hit**) / "He's My Sunny Boy"	Motown 1156	10/14/69

Florence Ballard (1968)

TITLE	LABEL	RELEASE DATE
"It Doesn't Matter How I Say It (It's What I Say That Matters)" / "Goin' out of My Head"	ABC 11074	04/1968
"Love Ain't Love"/ "Forever Faithful"	ABC 11144	09/1968

ALBUMS

The Supremes

TITLE	LABEL	RELEASE DATE
Meet the Supremes	Motown 606	12/1963
Where Did Our Love Go?	Motown 621	01/1965
A Bit of Liverpool	Motown 623	10/1964
The Supremes Sing Country and Western and Pop	Motown 625	02/1965
More Hits by the Supremes	Motown 627	07/1965
We Remember Sam Cooke	Motown 629	05/1965
Supremes at the Copa	Motown 636	11/1965
Merry Christmas	Motown 638	11/1965
I Hear a Symphony	Motown 643	02/1966
The Supremes a Go-Go	Motown 649	08/1966
The Supremes Sing Holland-Dozier-Holland	Motown 650	01/1967
The Supremes Sing Rodgers & Hart	Motown 659	08/1967

Diana Ross and the Supremes

TITLE	LABEL	RELEASE DATE
Greatest Hits Volumes I and II	Motown 663	08/1967
Reflections	Motown 665	08/1968

Florence Ballard

TITLE	LABEL	RELEASE DATE
The Supreme Florence Ballard	Spectrum	09/18/01

Appendix 2

Excerpts from Florence Ballard's Legal Case Against Motown Records et al.

FROM COMPLAINT filed by Florence Ballard Chapman, a/k/a Florence Ballard, Plaintiff vs. Diana Ross, individually, Mary Wilson, individually, Cindy Birdsong, individually, Jean Terrell, individually, Berry Gordy, Jr., individually and as President of International Management Company and Motown Record Corporation, Michael Roshkind, Ralph Seltzer, International Management Company, Motown Record Corporation, and [John or Jane] Does 1 through 10, inclusive, jointly and several. Filed by Attorney Gerald K. Dent of Patmon Young & Kirk Professional Corporation before Wayne County Circuit Court Judge Edward F. Bell, February 2, 1971, General Civil Act Case No. 173852.

1. The true names or capacities, whether individual, corporate, associate or otherwise, of defendants . . . 1 through 10, inclusive, are unknown to Plaintiff, who therefore sues said defendants by such fictitious names. Plaintiff is informed and believes and therefore alleges that each of [these] defendants is responsible in some manner for the events and happenings herein referred to, and caused damages . . . thereby to Plaintiff as herein alleged; by whose names are not now known to Plaintiff and she therefore sues said Defendants by such fictitious names and she will amend this Complaint to show the true names and capacities when the same has been ascertained.

2. Plaintiff is and has been for many years a resident of the City of Detroit . . . Plaintiff is a performing artist and entertainer, widely regarded as a highly skilled and outstanding performer and entertainer . . . in the entertainment and musical field. . . .

13. Commencing in the year 1960, Miss Ballard, who was then 17 years of age, became associated with Defendant Berry Gordy, Jr. in a business way as it related to Miss Ballard's skills as a female vocalist and with Defendant Berry Gordy, Jr. as President of the two Defendant corporations.

14. On or about January 15, 1961, in the City of Detroit, while still a minor, Miss Ballard entered into her first recording agreement with Defendant Motown; however, she was never given a copy of that agreement nor was she represented by an attorney of her own choice nor anyone else outside of Defendants Berry Gordy, Jr., Motown, and International. . . .

15. That on or about January 15, 1961 in the City of Detroit, while still a minor, Miss Ballard entered into a management agreement with Defendant International [Management], then known as Berry Gordy Jr. Enterprises, Inc.; however, she was never given a copy of that agreement nor was she represented by an attorney of her own choice nor anyone else outside of Defendants Berry Gordy, Jr., Motown, and International.

16. At no time before nor after Miss Ballard entered into the said recording agreement and the management agreement did she ever read the said agreements or know or understand the contents and terms of either of them nor the terms of years that the agreements were to last.

17. At the time Miss Ballard signed the agreements . . . Defendant Berry Gordy, Jr. represented to Miss Ballard that she need not worry or be concerned about her agreements and the contents, terms and conditions of them and that he, Berry Gordy, Jr., would take care of her, her financial, professional, business and personal affairs and her singing and performing career.

18. In reliance upon Defendant Berry Gordy, Jr.'s representations . . ., Miss Ballard did not demand copies of said agreements and placed complete faith and trust in Defendant Berry Gordy, Jr.'s representatives and allowed him to handle and manage her financial, business, professional affairs and her personal affairs and her singing and professional career. . . .

20. At no time before signing nor during the term of existence of said recording agreements with Defendant Motown and the management agreement with Defendants International . . . did Miss Ballard know the nature and the exact amount and extent of the compensation and monies that she was lawfully entitled to receive from . . . her recording agreement . . . as an internationally per-

forming female vocal artist and entertainer. . . . none of the Defendants ever counseled, advised, informed nor gave her any details regarding the compensation that she was rightfully and lawfully entitled to receive from the various and many services that she performed as an internationally renowned entertainer and female vocalist; she relied upon the good faith of all of the Defendants to see that all of her affairs were taken care of by them and properly managed by them for her benefit; she justifiably at the time relied upon them to see that she received all of the monies and compensation that she was and would be entitled to; and the Defendants knew that they had her complete reliance and trust. . . .

25. . . . By the terms of such agreement . . . Defendant International was to negotiate the terms of any and all contracts on behalf of Miss Ballard; and to exert itself to the best of its endeavors and efforts and to the utmost of its skill, power, and ability to represent her in all branches of the entertainment field.

26. . . . [By] the terms of such agreement . . . Defendant International was to use its best efforts to advise Miss Ballard in connection with all phases of her career and to counsel her in connection with all selection of engagements, and choice of material, public relations, financial affairs and in the negotiations of all agreements affecting Miss Ballard's career.

27. That from the beginning of her association with Defendants . . . Miss Ballard devoted herself to the performing acts and received widespread popularity and international acclaim.

28. That during the time that Miss Ballard was a member of the Supremes, she performed numerous engagements at the most exclusive nightclubs, supper clubs, television programs and public facilities through the United States and in foreign countries earning substantial amounts of monies.

29. That during the times that Miss Ballard was performing as a member of the Supremes, Defendant Berry Gordy, Jr. was functioning in the role of personal manager, representative and advisor for the group; Defendant Berry Gordy, Jr. was to take care of all financial affairs for Miss Ballard.

30. That during all times that Miss Ballard was performing and associated with the Supremes up to and including February, 1968, Defendant Berry Gordy, Jr., in his own individual capacity and as personal manager, representative and advisor to the Supremes and as President of the corporate defendants International and Motown, represented to Miss Ballard that he was her trusted friend and that he would manage, promote, develop and protect her professional career; and that he would make sure that she received her rightful and due compensation earned by herself from the various personal and television appearances;

that he would take it upon himself to make sure that she received all of the royalties and monies earned by herself from merchandising rights and the sale of phonograph records; that he represented to her that all the monies earned by her were being set aside for her benefit in a separate account and trust; and that he would make wise and prudent investments on her behalf; further Defendant Berry Gordy, Jr. represented to Miss Ballard that he would diligently take all steps necessary to protect, enhance and preserve the numerous rights of Miss Ballard.

31. Miss Ballard relied upon the representations made by Defendant Berry Gordy, Jr. in his individual capacity and in his capacity as President of corporate Defendants International and Motown and placed complete and full trust in him as a friend and in his abilities as a personal manager. . . .

32. That at no time from 1960 up to February, 1968 had Miss Ballard been informed by any of the Defendants or their agents of the exact amount of compensation and monies she was entitled to receive. . . .

34. . . . In the year 1966, the Supremes as a group earned in excess of One Million Dollars for personal appearances at public entertainment facilities; the monies earned from these personal appearances were handled, collected and held in trust by Defendant International and Defendant Berry Gordy, Jr., in his individual capacity, in his capacity as President of Defendant International and in his capacity as personal manager, advisor and representative of the Supremes and as personal and individual manager, advisor and representative of Miss Ballard.

35. . . . In the year 1967, the Supremes . . . obtained booking in engagements for 1967 with guaranteed sums in excess of $1,666,633.94 to be earned from personal appearances. . . .

36. . . . Sometime during the year of 1967, the Supremes obtained advanced booking engagements for personal appearances at public entertainment facilities for the year 1968 in excess of 3/4 Million Dollars. . . .

37. During the years 1966, 1967, and 1968 Defendants International entered into contractual agreements with the public on behalf of the Supremes and Miss Ballard . . .; however, Miss Ballard never received copies of said contractual arrangements but Defendant International obtained copies of them.

38. At the time that Miss Ballard entered into the music business, she was without knowledge in all areas of the music and entertainment business and particularly the record industry, as is evidenced by the facts that:

   a) Miss Ballard had not finished high school and had not acquired any formal or actual training in business dealings;

b) At no time during the signing of the said agreements and during her professional career with Defendants Motown and International was Miss Ballard ever represented by an attorney of her own choosing and was in fact, instructed by Defendant Berry Gordy, Jr. not to do so;

c) Miss Ballard never read any of the said agreements, nor, with her limited experience in such matters, would she have understood the content therein, if she had read them . . .

39. . . . Defendant Diana Ross . . . held herself out as a partner to Miss Ballard.

40. During sometime in late 1967, and on diverse times thereafter, the Defendants herein, their servants and agents, in conspiracy with each other, secretly, subversively and maliciously planned and plotted and took steps to oust Miss Ballard from the Supremes. . . .

41. During the latter part of 1967, Miss Ballard began to realize that the harmonious relationship existing between the members of the Supremes was beginning to deteriorate and Miss Ballard became the constant subject of unjustified and unwarranted criticism from Defendants Diana Ross and Berry Gordy, Jr., regarding her professional performance as a female vocalist with the Supremes. . . .

42. During the latter part of 1967, Miss Ballard was repeatedly told by Defendant Berry Gordy, Jr. that she was not singing properly and that her performances were having ill-effects upon the general quality of performance of the Supremes.

43. Sometime during the latter portion of 1967, while the Supremes were performing in Las Vegas, Nevada, Defendant Berry Gordy, Jr. advised Miss Ballard that she could not perform with the said group because she was not singing well.

44. At all times that Defendant Berry Gordy, Jr. and Defendant Diana Ross were representing to Miss Ballard that her performances were affecting the Supremes adversely, Defendant Berry Gordy, Jr. and Defendant Diana Ross were secretly conspiring and plotting to oust Miss Ballard from the Supremes. . . .

45. At all times that Defendant Berry Gordy, Jr. was representing to Miss Ballard that she wasn't performing in a professional manner with the Supremes, he and Defendant Diana Ross were secretly planning to oust Miss Ballard from the Supremes and replace her with one Cindy Birdsong.

46. At all times that Defendants Berry Gordy, Jr. and Diana Ross, their servants and agents, were secretly conspiring to wrongfully oust Miss Ballard from the Supremes, Miss Ballard had valid and binding contracts with Defendants Motown and International regarding her relationship with the Supremes.

47. At all times that Defendants Berry Gordy, Jr. and Diana Ross made representations to Miss Ballard that her singing performance with the Supremes was not

well enough professionally and their representations that Miss Ballard's singing performances with the Supremes were having adverse effects upon the group, Defendants Berry Gordy, Jr. and Diana Ross knew that the said representations were false and fraudulent. . . .

48. . . . For a period of two and a half years, from 1964 to 1967, the Supremes became the top female vocal group in the United States and elsewhere and their records began selling at a phenomenal rate. . . .

53. . . . During 1967, the Supremes were selling over 750,000 phonograph records per month. . . .

54. During 1964 through 1967, while Miss Ballard and the Supremes were selling records at a phenomenal rate, Miss Ballard was without knowledge of the amount and the extent of monies and royalties that she was entitled to, although Defendants Motown, International, Berry Gordy, Jr., their agents and servants knew the exact amount that Miss Ballard was entitled to at that particular time and they also knew that she was entitled to vast amounts of money in the form of future royalties, earnings, and other monies.

55. During the same period of time from 1964 to 1967, the group name "Supremes" had established goodwill that was valued well in excess of One Million Dollars.

56. . . . the Defendants, their servants and agents, in furtherance of their conspiracy to fraudulently and wrongfully remove and oust Miss Ballard from the Supremes, purposefully, maliciously, subversively, fraudulently and wrongfully concealed from Miss Ballard the extent and amounts of personal properties and monies that the corporate Defendants International and Motown had possession of belonging to Miss Ballard; the Defendants also purposefully concealed from Miss Ballard the enormous extent of the vast amounts of monies that Miss Ballard was entitled to in the form of future royalties and earnings from the sales of . . . single records and albums. . . .

57. The Defendants, their servants and agents were familiar with the music business and in particular the record and management business, while knowing that Miss Ballard was inexperienced and completely unaware of the final and business aspects of the music business. The Defendants also knew that Miss Ballard would rely upon their representations. . . .

59. On or about July of 1967, the Defendants . . . in furtherance of their conspiracy to oust Miss Ballard from the Supremes . . . dispatched Michael Roshkind to travel from New York City. . . to Detroit with instructions to contact Miss Ballard and to induce her to sign certain papers allowing the Defendants to remove her from the Supremes.

60. In furtherance of said conspiracy, on or about the month of July, 1967, Defendant Michael Roshkind arrived in Detroit and checked into a hotel known as the Northland Inn . . . that after arriving at the hotel, Defendant Michael Roshkind summoned Miss Ballard to meet with him.

61. On or about July 28, 1967, Miss Ballard went to the said hotel to meet with Defendant Michael Roshkind . . . Roshkind fraudulently represented that she was not entitled to receive any monies from Defendants Berry Gordy, Jr., International, Diana Ross or Motown in the form of present monies or future royalties or earnings; he also represented to Miss Ballard that her performances with the Supremes were having adverse effects upon the group's popularity and that it would be in "everyone's" best interest for her to allow the Defendants to remove Miss Ballard from the group; in a further attempt to fraudulently and falsely induce Miss Ballard to allow the Defendants to remove her from the Supremes . . . Roshkind represented to Miss Ballard that Defendant Motown would pay Miss Ballard $2,500 per year for six years for allowing the Defendants to remove Miss Ballard from the Supremes; Defendant Michael Roshkind also represented to Miss Ballard that none of the Defendants had any present or future obligations to her, financial or otherwise, and the Defendants were doing her a benevolent favor by offering her $2,500 for the next six years.

62. . . . Miss Ballard was fraudulently induced to sign the document. . . .

63. At the time that Defendant Michael Roshkind was making the said false and fraudulent representations to Miss Ballard, he knew that Miss Ballard had none of her monies in her possession and that her monies were under the exclusive control of the Defendants and that Miss Ballard was merely receiving a meager allowance from the Defendants.

64. Thereafter, Miss Ballard retained an attorney who then contacted the Defendants concerning the Supplemental Agreement; the Defendants, their servants and agents then had discussions and negotiations with Miss Ballard's attorney from August 1967 to February 1968 regarding the setting aside of the . . . agreement and replacing it with another; however, during all of this period of time the Defendants, their servants and agents, successfully concealed their conspiracy to wrongly, maliciously and unlawfully oust Miss Ballard from the Supremes from both Miss Ballard and her attorney.

65. On or about the 22nd day of February 1968, the Defendants completed their last substantive and substantial act in furtherance of their conspiracy to fraudulently oust Miss Ballard from the Supremes by having her enter into a purported general release agreement removing her from the Supremes and paying

her meager and grossly inadequate sums of monies as it related to her various rights.

66. During all the . . . period of the time of the conspiracy to oust Miss Ballard from the Supremes . . . Defendants, their servants and agents repeatedly represented to Miss Ballard that her professional performances were no longer the high caliber of the other two Supremes . . . that Miss Ballard's performances with the Supremes were having and would continue to have adverse effects upon the general performance of the Supremes and upon the caliber and standard of the Supremes' performances and was and would adversely affect the general public's acceptance of the group and the sale of the phonograph records; Defendants, their servants and agents knew that these representations were false and fraudulent; the said representations were made with the malicious intent that Miss Ballard would rely upon the same, which Miss Ballard did; the intent and purpose of these representations was in furtherance of the . . . conspiracy to maliciously, wrongfully and fraudulently oust Miss Ballard from the Supremes.

67. Miss Ballard was not able to uncover the true nature of the malicious conspiracy to oust her from the Supremes until the latter part of 1968.

68. This conspiracy violated the laws of the State of Michigan and has succeeded in causing irreparable damage to Miss Ballard and the public.

69. As a consequence of the conspiracy to oust Miss Ballard from the Supremes and to wreck and destroy her professional career, Miss Ballard has suffered damage to her non-entertainment and business interests, damage to her ability to receive fees from product endorsements and publicity appearances, damages to her professional career as a female vocalist, and other damages, all in excess of One and One-half Million Dollars. . . .

94. On diverse occasions . . . Defendant Motown, its servants and agents, maliciously and intentionally failed to devote to Miss Ballard's career the same degree and extent of promotion, exploitation, sales efforts and advertisement consistent to what Defendants provided and undertook for Defendant Diana Ross.

95. During the existence of said agreement, Defendant Motown, its servants and agents, maliciously and intentionally, has failed and continue to fail and refuse to account, to make proper and adequate payment of monies due and owing to Miss Ballard as required under the recording agreement.

96. Defendant Motown failed and/or refused to permit Miss Ballard the right to inspect and/or audit Defendant's books and records as the said books and records pertained to monies that Miss Ballard was entitled to receive pursuant to said recording agreement. . . . Defendant Motown has failed and/or refused to furnish proper and required accounting statements of the monies that Miss

Ballard was entitled to receive pursuant to the terms and conditions of said agreement.

97. Defendant Motown has refused, and continuously refused during the time of the existence of the said agreement, up to and including the time of the filing of this complaint to pay over monies due and owing to Miss Ballard from the sale of tapes and cartridges mechanically reproduced from master recordings embodying Miss Ballard's performance.

98. . . . Defendant Motown from 1964 until the present time has received over $10,000,000.00 from the sale of tapes and other cartridges embodying reproductions of musical compositions of the "Supremes" and Miss Ballard.

99. Defendant Motown from the year 1964 to the present has rendered false and fraudulent accounts to Miss Ballard grossly understating the royalties belonging to her.

100. On information and belief, Defendant Motown from 1964 to the present time has fraudulently, falsely and excessively overcharged Miss Ballard for the cost of arrangements, copying, accompaniments and other costs relating to each master recording embodying Miss Ballard's performances.

101. . . . Defendant Motown, its servants and agents from 1964 to the present time have secretly concealed from Miss Ballard the true costs and charges properly allocable to herself by Defendant Motown.

102. Defendant Motown fraudulently and falsely and excessively offset said costs referred to hereof in the cause of action and wrongly offset said costs against royalties, earnings and other monies properly due and belonging to Miss Ballard.

103. During the same period of time . . . Defendant Motown and Miss Ballard agreed that she was to receive certain compensations for making television and radio commercials.

104. . . . Defendant Motown failed to pay unto Miss Ballard the proper sums of monies that she was entitled to receive pursuant to the services she rendered. . . .

105. That at the time of the execution of the said agreement and during all of the time of its existence up to and including the time of the filing of this complaint, Defendant Motown agreed to grant foreign licenses for the purpose of manufacturing and selling phonograph records embodying the performances of Miss Ballard.

106. . . . Defendant Motown's foreign licenses were inadequate in that, among other things, they failed to properly and adequately manufacture, distribute, market, exploit and sell phonograph records which embodied Miss Ballard's performances.

107. The foreign licenses selected by Defendant Motown was [sic] done in a grossly negligent manner.

108. Defendant Motown should have and would have realized that the said foreign licensees were deficient and inadequate in capabilities to sufficiently manufacture, market, exploit and sell said phonograph records.

109. Defendant Motown should have and could have known about the deficiencies of said foreign licensees if they had properly investigated the foreign licensees before entering into said agreements with them.

110. As a result of Defendant Motown's lack of diligence and care . . . Miss Ballard has lost vast and substantial amounts of money and loss of rights.

111. Defendant Motown further breached terms of the said contract by engaging in the conspiracy to oust Miss Ballard from the "Supremes" as referred to in Count 1 of this complaint.

112. Defendant Motown breached the terms and conditions of said agreement and violated their duties to Miss Ballard by engaging in the conspiracy to fraudulently defraud Miss Ballard of the vast sums of money that she was entitled to receive. . . .

113. That as a result of the above described acts and omissions, breach of express provisions of said agreement, breach of fiduciary and special relationships, Defendant Motown has succeeded in causing irreparable damage to Miss Ballard and the public.

114. As a consequence of the acts and/or omissions on the part of the Defendants regarding their obligations under the said agreement, Miss Ballard has suffered and will suffer damage to her non-entertainment business interest, damage to her ability to receive fees and benefits from product endorsement and publicity appearances, and other damages in excess of $2,000,000.00. . . .

116. At all times from and after the effective date of August 10, 1964, the date of the agreement between Miss Ballard and Defendant International and continuously throughout the entire terms thereof up to and including the date of the filing of this complaint, Miss Ballard fully and faithfully performed her obligations. . . .

117. That at the time that Defendant International was acting in the capacity as Miss Ballard's personal representative, agent, advisor, business and financial advisor and as business manager as it related to the total aspect of her professional career and personal affairs, Defendant Berry Gordy, Jr. in his capacities as the President of Motown, the President of International and in his individual capacity, was acting as Miss Ballard's personal manager.

118. The said management agreement was drafted by the Defendant International and their attorneys without discussion or consultation with Miss Ballard or any attorney representing her interests.

119. The said management agreement gave Defendant International almost complete and total control and direction over Miss Ballard as it related to her professional career; among other things, International was to be her exclusive manager, representative, advisor, agent, as it related to all phases of her professional and entertainment career; and generally, Defendant International was to exert itself to the best of its endeavors and to the utmost of its skill, power, and ability and to represent Miss Ballard in all branches of the entertainment field.

120. By the terms of the said agreements and by virtue of the fact that Defendant Berry Gordy, Jr., in his many roles and capacities as Miss Ballard's personal manager and the President of International and controlling stockholder of International, Defendant International enjoyed and occupied a special fiduciary relationship with Miss Ballard.

121. By reason of the special confidence and fiduciary relationship, it was the duty and obligation of Defendant International, its respective officers, attorneys, agents, accountants and servants to exercise the utmost good faith, trust and care in the handling and managing of Miss Ballard's financial and business affairs and her professional career.

122. Defendant International had fiduciary duties to Miss Ballard to exercise the utmost candor, fidelity and honesty in handling all of her affairs and to observe the highest and strictest form of integrity pertaining to Miss Ballard; and to refrain from abusing such confidence and fiduciary relationship and from obtaining any advantage to itself or for the benefit of others at the expense of Miss Ballard.

123. During the terms of said agreement Defendant International, on diverse occasions and continually up to and including the date of this complaint, intentionally, maliciously and subversively failed to treat Miss Ballard's career in the same manner consistent with Defendant Diana Ross' career; Defendant International failed to promote and use its best efforts in furtherance of Miss Ballard's career as it did with Defendant Diana Ross' career.

124. .... Defendant International wrongfully breached their fiduciary duties in representing Defendant Diana Ross to the detriment and harm of Miss Ballard; and in representing its own interests contrary to the best interests of Miss Ballard.

125. Defendant International was under obligation pursuant to said agreement to use its best efforts to promote Miss Ballard's career and to obtain personal engagements for her.

126. Defendant International, in breaching its obligations as Miss Ballard's exclusive business manager and personal representative, refused, failed and neglected to obtain personal engagements for Miss Ballard to exploit her talents.

127. Pursuant to said agreement, Defendant International was obliged to use its best efforts to advise Miss Ballard in connection with all phases of her career and to counsel her in connection with the selection of engagements, public relations, financial affairs and in the negotiation of all agreements affecting Miss Ballard's career.

128. . . . On diverse occasions, from August 10, 1964 up to and including the time of filing of this complaint, Defendant International failed to use its best efforts in negotiating agreements with the public on behalf of Miss Ballard; Defendant did, in fact, make agreements with third parties as agent for Miss Ballard for its own benefit and self-enrichment.

129. . . . On diverse occasions, from August 10, 1964 up to and including the time and filing of this complaint, Defendant International failed to properly and adequately and honestly advise, direct and guide Miss Ballard's career, financial affairs and business interests in a reasonable and prudent manner; Defendant International subversively, maliciously, fraudulently and without justification rendered imprudent and purposeful misguidance to Miss Ballard as it related to her professional career, financial affairs and business interests.

130. . . . on diverse occasions, from August 10, 1964 on to and including the time of filing of this complaint, Defendant International rendered Miss Ballard harmful advice and counsel regarding her professional career not for her benefit but for the benefit of Defendant International, of the corporate Defendant Motown and Defendant Diana Ross.

131. . . . Defendant International rendered false and fraudulent accounting understating monies payable to Miss Ballard on personal engagements where Miss Ballard performed as an artist.

132. Defendant International had the obligation to act as trustee of Miss Ballard's funds which she had earned and was entitled to earn from personal engagements; on diverse occasions Defendant International misrepresented to Miss Ballard the extent and amounts of monies that Defendant International was holding as trustee. . . .

134. Defendant International's relationship with Defendant Motown conflicted with the expressed obligations that Defendant International owed to Miss Ballard; Defendant International operated in the self-interest of itself and Defendant Motown to the detriment of Miss Ballard during all of the aforementioned times obtaining large and vast sums of monies for its own economic interest and for

Defendant Motown in direct violation of the many and various fiduciary obligations owing to Miss Ballard. . . .

165. . . . Defendants International, Berry Gordy, Jr., and Diana Ross . . . falsely and fraudulently represented and stated to Miss Ballard's attorney, for the purpose of inducing Miss Ballard to execute said purported releases, that:

a) Defendant International had accounted to her for all sums due or to become due to her as an artist on accounts of personal appearances from the beginning of the term of the original management agreement and all subsequent agreements to the date of the purported release agreement, except in the sum of $20,195.06;

b) That all items of income and items of expense and various items of every other description were correct in every respect and that she had received complete and accurate accounts of royalties and savings pursuant to said management agreement;

c) That it was in the best interest of Miss Ballard to waive the right to receive any sums as a co-owner of the name "The Supremes". . . .

166. At the said time that Defendant International offered and agreed to pay Miss Ballard a total of $20,195.06 for her various rights and assets . . . Defendant International knew that she was entitled to vast sums of monies and earnings far in excess of said offered sum; however, Defendant International, Defendant Berry Gordy, Jr. and Defendant Michael Roshkind, Defendant Ralph Seltzer, Defendant Diana Ross, their servants and agents, purposefully concealed these facts from Miss Ballard, knowing full well Miss Ballard and her attorney did not know the extent of the value of her various rights and would rely upon their representations.

167. . . . At the time that Defendants, their servants and agents, made said false and fraudulent misrepresentations, the value of Miss Ballard's various rights and assets pursuant to the various management contracts . . . was in excess of One Million Dollars.

168. At the time that Defendants Motown, Gordy, Seltzer, Roshkind, their servants and agents, represented to Miss Ballard's attorney that all of her various rights pursuant to the . . . recording agreements was only worth $134,804.94, Defendants had full knowledge of the fact that the sum offered by them to Miss Ballard was grossly inadequate as it related to the vast amount of monies that she was entitled to receive. Defendants also knew that Miss Ballard and her attorney would rely upon their representations.

169. . . . At the time that Defendants, their servants and agents, made said false and fraudulent misrepresentations, the value of Miss Ballard's various rights and

assets pursuant to the various recording contracts . . . was in excess of One Million Dollars.

170. Defendants Motown, Berry Gordy, Jr., Roshkind, Seltzer, their servants and agents, fraudulently and falsely concealed from Miss Ballard and her attorney the fact that she had never been paid or received any monies whatsoever from the sale of cartridges and other tapes.

174. . . . Defendants fraudulently, maliciously and subversively concealed from Miss Ballard and her attorney the true nature and extent of the monetary value and goodwill of the name "The Supremes."

175. The said Defendants, their servants and agents, did not offer nor did they ever pay Miss Ballard any monies or compensation for her co-ownership in the trade and business named The Supremes; and these acts and/or omissions, on the part of the Defendants herein, were done maliciously, subversively and fraudulently and in violation of all of their various . . . fiduciary duties and obligations.

176. The purported general release agreement . . . did not give Miss Ballard any . . . monies regarding her relinquishing and waiving all rights that she had to use the name "The Supremes." . . .

178. On or about February 22, 1968, Harold Noveck and David G. Hertzberg, attorneys for Defendants Motown, International, Berry Gordy, Jr. and Diana Ross negligently mailed three checks to Attorney Leonard A. Baun instead of to Miss Ballard, purportedly being sums of monies that the Defendants were to pay pursuant to said general release agreement. . . .

179. As a result of Defendants negligently giving said checks to Attorney Leonard A. Baun instead of to Miss Ballard, Miss Ballard never actually received the said checks; and Leonard A. Baun subsequently converted various of the said sums to his own use to the detriment of Miss Ballard.

180. The said checks that were to be payable to Miss Ballard as follows:
    a) Supremes Vocal Group $20,195.06
    b) Diana Ross and the Supremes $5,000
    c) Motown Record Corporation $134,804.94 . . .

202. The acts of misconduct on the part of all of the Defendants . . . , their servants and agents, caused Miss Ballard extreme emotional trauma, resulting in her experiencing severe psychological stress, causing her to experience deep mental anguish, depressing states of anxiety and emotional and mental distress. As a further result of all of the Defendants' conspiracies and various intentional acts of misconduct directed at Miss Ballard, she had undergone severe and painful personality changes. Her personality has changed from a very congenial nature to one that causes her at different and various periods of time to be extremely

nervous, highly irritable at the slightest and imaginary provocation. Miss Ballard has undergone changes in her personality from one of an outgoing, pleasant personality to one where during various periods of time she lapses into extreme states of withdrawal from society unto herself. At various periods of time, Miss Ballard has experienced distressful and abnormal amounts of fear and apprehension regarding people, causing her to manifest, at different times, paranoiac tendencies; all of these experiences, changes and ill-effects upon Miss Ballard's personal, mental, psychic, emotional stability and personality and well-being are the direct result of all the Defendants' intentional and malicious acts of misconduct . . . and these injuries and damages to Miss Ballard are past, present and future. . . .

207. The trade name "The Supremes" was a worthless partnership asset at the beginning. From 1961 to 1968 the name "The Supremes" gained phenomenal commercial value and goodwill as the result of the joint effort of Ross-Wilson-Ballard.

208. During the period of time that the group name "The Supremes" was made valuable, Ross-Wilson-Ballard were partners sharing equally in profits and losses while performing as entertainers under the group name.

209. During this same period of time the trade name was also the business name of Ross-Wilson-Ballard, such as having their bank accounts in the name of "The Supremes." . . .

214. On or about February 22, 1968, Defendants Motown, International, Berry Gordy, Jr. and Diana Ross, their servants and agents, falsely and fraudulently in the purported release agreement . . . represented to Miss Ballard, amongst other things, that
A) The name "The Supremes" was property owned by Defendant Motown and not Ross-Wilson-Ballard.
B) Miss Ballard had no rights, title or interest in the name "The Supremes."
C) Miss Ballard never had any interest in the ownership of the name "The Supremes" . . .

219. . . . Since Ross-Wilson-Ballard's entry into the partnership . . . Defendants Mary Wilson and Diana Ross have continually carried on the partnership under the name "The Supremes."

220. . . . Since on or about February 22, 1968, Defendants Diana Ross and Mary Wilson have taken and appropriated for their own use receipts and proceeds from said partnership business, the continued use and exploitation of the partnership name and assets, and sums of money greatly exceeding the proportions to which each of them were entitled. . . .

227. As a result of Miss Ballard's skill and competence as a singer and entertainer, in conjunction with the skills of Defendants Diana Ross and Mary Wilson, under the trade name "The Supremes," substantial monies, benefits and prestige accrued to the group, thereby creating valuable goodwill associated with the trade name. . . .

230. . . . Defendants Motown, International, and Berry Gordy, Jr. fraudulently, falsely, maliciously and internationally misrepresented the following:

   a) That the trade name "The Supremes" was originated and owned by said Defendant Motown;

   b) That Miss Ballard, individually, had no rights, title, ownership or interest in said trade name;

   c) That the trade name, "The Supremes," was the exclusive property of said Defendant Motown;

   d) That Miss Ballard at no time had any rights, title, ownership or interest in the trade name, individually, or as co-owners with Defendants Diana Ross and Mary Wilson . . .

232. . . . Defendants Motown, International, and Berry Gordy, Jr. permitted others to use and perform under the name "The Supremes" . . . the persons who performed under said trade name were Defendants Cindy Birdsong and Jean Terrell. . . .

238. . . . Defendants Motown, International, Berry Gordy, Jr., Cindy Birdsong and Jean Terrell have and continue to do irreparable harm to Miss Ballard's rights, title, ownership and interest in the trade name "The Supremes."

Sources

NEWSPAPERS

Detroit Free Press: 05/18/69, 07/03/69, 09/02/72, 09/03/72, 11/12/72,
 11/19/72, 04/01/73, 04/04/73, 04/05/73, 04/07/73, 01/16/75,
 07/03/75, 07/21/98, 05/25/99
Detroit News: 08/07/56, 05/27/60, 09/02/72, 09/03/72, 09/04/72,
 09/07/72, 05/19/84
Los Angeles Times: 02/23/76

MAGAZINES

Detroit Magazine: 10/20/68
Jet Magazine: 02/20/75, 05/15/00
Look Magazine: 05/03/66, 10/19/71

INTERVIEWS (IN PERSON, VIA TELEPHONE, OR VIA E-MAIL)

Alan Abrams, Billy Ballard, Florence Ballard, Linda Ballard, Katherine
 Ballard, Pat Ballard, Michelle Ballard Chapman, Nicole Ballard
 Chapman, Pat Cosby, Michael Hathaway, Florence Lollis, Alastair
 Londonderry, Jim Lopes, Weldon A. McDougal III, Roger Pearson,
 Katherine Anderson Schaffner, Andrew Skurow, Harry Weinger, Mary
 Wilson. Other interviewees requested anonymity.

Court Papers

The People of the State of Michigan vs. Reginald Harding, June 11, 1960, Detroit Recorder's Court

Chapman vs. Baun, Wayne County Circuit Court

232 N.W.2d 621, 395 Mich. 28, *In the Matter of the Complaint against Leonard A. Baun before the State Bar Grievance Board, Appellant.* No. 3. Supreme Court of Michigan, September 8, 1975, P. 621–629

In the Matter of Leonard A. Baun, a Member of the State Bar of Michigan, Appellant. No. 32207-A, Decided April 12, 1979.

Ballard vs. Ross et al, Wayne County Circuit Court

Other Official Papers

Florence Ballard Death Certificate, #2352, City of Detroit, Michigan.

Florance Ballard Chapman Autopsy Report, #A76-358, Wayne County, Michigan

Books

Ballard, Maxine. *The True Story of Florence Ballard.* Detroit: Precious4Max, Inc., 2007.

Benjaminson, Peter. *The Story of Motown.* New York: Grove Press, 1979.

Bianco, David. *Heat Wave: The Motown Fact Book.* Ann Arbor, MI: Pierian Press, 1988.

Gaar, Gillian G. *She's a Rebel: The History of Women in Rock 'n' Roll.* New York: Seal Press, 2002.

George, Nelson. *Where Did Our Love Go?: The Rise and Fall of the Motown Sound.* New York: St. Martin's Press, 1985.

Gordy, Berry. *To Be Loved: The Music, the Magic, the Memories of Motown.* New York: Warner Books, 1994.

Posner, Gerald. *Motown: Music, Sex, Money, and Power.* New York: Random House, 2002.

Ritz, David. *Divided Soul: The Life of Marvin Gaye*. New York: McGraw-Hill, 1985.

Ross, Diana. *Secrets of a Sparrow: Memoirs*. New York: Villard Books, 1993.

Spitz, Bob. *The Beatles: The Biography*. New York: Little, Brown, 2005.

Taraborrelli, J. Randy. *Call Her Miss Ross*. New York: Ballantine Books, 1991.

Taraborrelli, J. Randy. *Diana Ross: An Unauthorized Biography*. London: Sidgwick & Jackson, 2007.

Taylor, Marc. *The Original Marvelettes: Motown's Mystery Girl Group*. Jamaica, NY: Aloiv Publishing, 2004.

Turner, Tony. *All That Glittered: My Life with the Supremes*. New York: Dutton, 1990.

Waller, Don. *The Motown Story*. New York: Scribner's, 1985.

Williams, Otis. *Temptations*. New York: Cooper Square Press, 2002.

Wilson, Mary. *Dreamgirl: My Life as a Supreme*. New York: St. Martin's Press, 1986.

Wilson, Mary. *Dreamgirl and Supreme Faith*. New York: Cooper Square Press, 1999.

Wilson, Randall. *Forever Faithful! A Study of Florence Ballard and the Supremes*. San Francisco: Renaissance Sound & Publications, 1987.

Index